the Glory of God's LIGHT

Connect with God through His Light, Love, and Word

BROTHER RAYMOND

Ambassador International
GREENVILLE, SOUTH CAROLINA & BELFAST, NORTHERN IRELAND

www.ambassador-international.com

The Glory of God's Light

Connect with God Through His Light, Love, and Word
©2020 by Brother Raymond
All rights reserved

ISBN: 978-1-62020-911-0
eISBN: 978-1-62020-938-7

Cover Design and Page Layout by Hannah Nichols
eBook Conversion by Anna Riebe Raats

Unless otherwise indicated, Bible quotations are taken from the King James Version, copyright © Cambridge University Press and Oxford University Press 1961, 1970. All rights reserved.

Scripture quotations taken from the New King James Version®, copyright © 1982 by Thomas Nelson. Used by permission. All rights reserved.

Scripture quotations taken from THE MESSAGE, copyright © 1993, 1994, 1995, 1996, 2000, 2001, 2002 by Eugene H. Peterson. Used by permission of NavPress. All rights reserved. Represented by Tyndale House Publishers, Inc.

Scripture quotations taken from the Amplified® Bible, copyright © 2015 by The Lockman Foundation. Used by permission. www.Lockman.org.

AMBASSADOR INTERNATIONAL
Emerald House
411 University Ridge, Suite B14
Greenville, SC 29601, USA
www.ambassador-international.com

AMBASSADOR BOOKS
The Mount
2 Woodstock Link
Belfast, BT6 8DD, Northern Ireland, UK
www.ambassadormedia.co.uk

The colophon is a trademark of Ambassador, a Christian publishing company.

"All other books inform; the Bible both reforms and transforms. Yet, what the author achieves brilliantly in this book is not just the sincere scripting of his resolute convictions about the endless possibilities of being with God. It is, more importantly, how he allows the Holy Spirit of God to minister through him in crafting his words and shaping his ideas. In the end, what amounts is a simple, inspiring, and relatable account of the awesome power of the Holy Spirit to touch and change lives, however desperate the situation. This book will potentially reveal your story, help charge up your faith, and lead you to discover the endless possibilities of the kingdom of Heaven locked up within you."

—JAMES-EMMANUEL WANKI,
Commonwealth Alistair Berkeley Fellow, University of Oxford

"Brother Raymond's message is simple, powerful, and practical. He is a master of his piece. A must-read for those interested in bridging Christianity and personal development."

—DR. AKUMA SANINGONG,
Keynote Speaker, Entrepreneur, and Author

"Brother Raymond takes readers on a delightful journey into the glorious realms of God with this masterpiece."

—JOY OGEH-HUTFIELD,
Multi-Award-Winning Life and Business Coach, CEO Joy Transformation

"It is amazing to watch people you know grow in the grace of God and excel in wisdom and purpose. Raymond's words in this book are born out of a deep experience of his walk with God."

—GABRIEL M. ASHU-ARREY,
Founder and President, Global Entrepreneurship Corps

"A delightful awakening of the spirit that will renew your mindset. An enlightening and encouraging read for those who seek Christ and His companionship in daily life."

—CHRISTER EGON ECKERMANN,
Co-Founder, Snuti

"Author Brother Raymond explores three key areas needed for Christians to lead a transcendent life in a dark world—the glory of God's Light, the glory of God's Love, and the glory of God's Word. This simple but comprehensive study on each theme uses Scripture and personal accounts to explore the depths of each area. With the challenges of this life, each one of us will eventually attempt to counter the three "glory" areas in this book. Every believer can benefit from the reminder of God's power to live victoriously."

—ANDY SANDERS,
www.capturingthesupernatural.com

All glory to God, my Heavenly Father; Jesus Christ, my Lord and Savior; and the Holy Spirit, my Chief Strategist.

CONTENTS

AN ODE TO GOD

Great is the Lord of lords.

Great is the King of kings.

Great is the Lord of all creation,

Giver of life and inherent power.

Great is my God above all gods.

No faith without You,

No hope without You,

No love without You,

No peace without You.

Word is life and power;

Word is revelation to inspire;

Lose the life for You

To live for You forever.

Sanctified this tome by action;

Storms came as some turned their backs.

Made all tranquil in the isle,

Darkness loomed with blocked tracks.

Light shone so bright on the aisle

In the deep valley thrown off the butte,

Endured hardship holding on to your Word

No bitterness whilst others seemed jolly.

No tomfoolery but to always rejoice in the weird.

Once upon a time out of my mother's womb bare.

Came into my life and transformed my cord

To be an able minister of Your Word, my Lord.

ACKNOWLEDGMENTS

To my beautiful family—my darling wife, Margaret; our son, Evan; and our daughter, Zoey. Thank you for all your love.

My sincere gratitude goes out to Pastor Yvonne, Pastor Peter, Pastor Matthew, and Pastor Alain. Thank you for your guidance in the work of ministry and your labor of love.

To Andy Sanders, Cathy Sanders, and Jeff Pelton. Thank you for your assistance.

To Boma, James, Rita, Felicia, Stefania, John, Mariam, Gabriel, Joy, Azocha, Christer, Komme, and Akuma. Thank you for your support.

Special honors to my mom, Ziporah, and my late dad, Fritz. To my siblings, Geraldine, Nelly, George, Doreen, Eric, and their families, you all have been fantastic.

Hats off to my editor Katie Cruice Smith and the entire team at Ambassador International.

Lastly, to my wonderful readers, wherever you are in the world—I love you all. God bless you!

FOREWORD

I first met Raymond at Singleton Park Library in Swansea University, United Kingdom. I was in pursuit of my undergraduate degree. Raymond had come to Swansea to pursue a postgraduate degree. I have come to know him as a down-to-earth, gracious, cool, noble, and inspiring person.

My passion for Gospel music is aglow. It has made me love God more and more. Can I explain why I sing Gospel music? Gospel music is an expression of love. It is an act of godly worship. To me, Gospel music is all about sending a message of faith, hope, and love. It is intended to bless you.

One of my singles, "I Am Satisfied,"[1] truly inspires Raymond. The message in the song is that you can get fulfilment from walking with Jesus Christ. Jesus is available to be with you in your trials—and in the deepest abyss. You can count on Him. Without Him, we are empty.

Some people believe in God. Some others do not believe for many different reasons. If people all around the world worship God, appreciate His steadfast love and goodness, and meditate on His Word, don't you think we would be living in a much more glorious world?

Regardless of your geographical whereabouts, it is likely that tribulations will merge into your lane. When trouble strikes, to whom are you going to run? *The Glory of God's Light* is an exposé of God in the beauty of His Divine glory, eternity, love, and truth. It provides a weighty and rousing perspective

---

1 Boma Harry. The Parchment. Boma Music. I Am Satisfied (Single). 2017. Accessed January 3, 2018. https://www.youtube.com/watch?v=MnL1gw9ypiQ.

on how you can connect with God in three simple ways—His Light, His Love, and His Word.

—BOMA C. HARRY,

Gospel Music Singer

PREFACE

From Montreal to Toronto, Baltimore to Silicon Valley, São Paulo to Buenos Aires, Lagos to Douala, Kinshasa to Dakar, Baghdad to Damascus, Melbourne to Manila, Mumbai to Kabul, Seoul to Shanghai, Hamburg to Paris, Oslo to Belfast, Moscow to Istanbul, Dubai to Jerusalem, to wherever you are, I greet you in the name of Jesus Christ.

I am so delighted to share this book with you. It is an honor to share the Good News with you. God is the very Essence of our lives. He knew you before you were born. He is your Heavenly Father. I am asking you to explore connecting with God if you have not already done so.

Can you separate a branch from the vine? Can you separate a child from the mother? Can you separate human beings from God? Can you separate light from Light?

God is Light. One thing I know for sure is that I am born of God. I know He created me. He is my Source. I am a child of Light. For many years now, I have walked with Him. He has shown me what it means to walk in His Light.

I don't know any other way I could present myself to God than offering myself as a living sacrifice. God did not create me to live for myself. He created me to live for Him. Many people are stressed because they are living for themselves. The day I realized I was to live for Him, the stress was gone. I threw all my burdens on Him, and He takes care of me more than anyone else in the world.

Everyone in the world faces challenges—the super-rich, the middle class, the average joe, and the ordinary jane. Some of these challenges represent darkness. Darkness has taken some to the graves. Darkness has made the lives of some miserable.

Is your dream dead? Have you lost faith in yourself? What happened to your dream? All is not lost. In John 16:33, Jesus declared that there will be trials and sorrows on the earth, but you should cheer up because He overcame the world. There is hope for you.

My cherished brother or sister, there is nothing more glorious and fulfilling as having a great relationship with God. God can revive your dreams today. There are billions of people living in the world. The world yearns for the manifestation of God. No matter who you are or what you've done, let me tell you something: God loves you!

I can only imagine the pain and frustration that you have gone through or are going through—work stress, family problems, or personal issues. Who wouldn't be frustrated to be in any of these scenarios? Sometimes, it really hurts, and it feels like you are alone in a cave. You might be screaming inside, and it appears no one deeply understands your ordeal. I would like to encourage you to persevere because the situation is bound to change. The affliction is not permanent (2 Cor. 4:17).

My beloved friend, I also understand that there are some snags in your life that nobody knows about—deep emotional issues. When you are alone in your bedroom, your thoughts raging as fire, you may be feeling empty inside. Perhaps it appears things are turning topsy-turvy in your soul. You are silently screaming deep within. You are out there thinking, "God, where are You in all of this mess? I don't know what to do with my life!"

What overwhelms you? Your best friend's child died just like that. Your colleague's wife passed on after a terrible car accident. Your cousin lost her life unpredictably. "God, why?" This really makes you melancholy. Do these things negate God's presence? If you were looking for God, you would find

Him amid your woe—"a very present help" in times of need (Psa. 46:1). The Bible invites you to God's throne of grace to obtain compassion and find grace for your situation (Heb 4:16).

The context of God's grace simply means He gives you His unconditional love when you are in your cave. God does not charge you a dime for it. To receive His grace, you simply need to ask Him in prayer, and He will give it to you.

You might be asking yourself, "Does God really care about me?" God accepts everybody irrespective of marital status, race, color, age, health condition, creed, gender identity, genetic information, financial status, or sexual orientation. God does not condemn anybody. He loves the worst of the worst. He loves you more than a parent loves a child. He just wants to be a part of your life. Period!

Sometimes, it may seem as if your situation might be the problem. But it is often your reaction to the things that happen in your life that affects you the most. For example, you lost your job. You feel like everything has fallen apart. This is a painful situation because it appears your financial health is in jeopardy.

In John 16:33, Jesus urges you to take heart and bask in His peace, being encouraged, regardless of the trials and sorrows that you go through. Life is too short to get stuck in a rut.

This book gives you an opportunity to take a step back and reflect on God's grace. His grace creates an enabling environment to connect with Him. Don't get tempted to get discouraged. I pray for God's strength and peace to overwhelm you. All you need today is more of His grace to give you the victory over any inauspicious situation.

You may have been crestfallen by a repulsive situation. Maybe you are in a relationship, and your partner just walked out the door and is never coming back to you. You feel so terrible with your heartbreak battle. Your tears are piling up every night. You have lost your mind. Your heart is deeply bleeding. The storm is crushing you. You don't know what to do next.

But let me tell you something terrific. Jesus Christ is here. He wants to kiss your pain away. He knows and loves you. Would you allow Him to become your friend? Instead of focusing on your problem, can you set your gaze on Jesus for a moment?

But Who is this Jesus Christ? Jesus is the Son of God. Where does He live? He lives in Heaven. Where is Heaven? Heaven is far beyond the skies. How can you get to know Him? How can He solve your problems? Can you see the Light?

To receive Jesus Christ in your life, you must pray a simple prayer that you accept Him as your Lord and Savior, and you will be saved from all iniquities. What is iniquity? An iniquity is anything that is inconsistent with God's Word. What is God's Word? Jesus is God's Word made flesh—the Word incarnate (Jn. 1:14).

God's plan for you is such that you enjoy life and have a future filled with hope (Jer. 29:11). His plan for you is not that you stay hopeless or purposeless. My beloved friend, I don't know if you have lost all hope. Don't be discouraged. Trust God because He is the greatest Love of all. God bless you!

God's Word is Truth (Psa. 119:142; Eph. 1:13; Jn. 17:17). The knowledge of God's Truth leads you to a glorious experience with God. You can only achieve real freedom in your life by having an accurate knowledge of God's Word.

If your heart were flinty or lukewarm, it would be impossible to have a great relationship with God because there is a spiritual barricade between you and Him. This book shows you how to connect with God in three simple ways—through His light, by His love, and in His Word.

1

THE GLORY OF GOD'S LIGHT

Mighty God, Everlasting Father,

Thy Light is Truth.

Thy Light is sublime.

Thy Light is boundless.

Thy Light is glorious.

Thy Light shines in my spirit.

Thy Light shines in my soul.

Thy Light shines in my body.

Thy Light is joy.

Thy Light is life.

Thy Light endures forever.

Thy Light makes me clean.

Thy Light is righteousness.

Thy Light renews my mind.

Thy Light keeps me in perfect peace.

Thy Light shines in desolate places.

Thy Light brings me out of the woods.

Thy Light turns my shame to glory.

Thy Light makes my heart aglow.

Thy Light is the answer in the day of trouble.

I understand that it might be difficult for some people to have a great relationship with God. How do you connect with God if you barely know Him? It might be somewhat difficult to paint a picture of what each person's situation looks like. Obviously, people have been raised in distinctive spaces. If I were to wear my sociological lens for a minute, it would be safe to state that who we are reflects the steady acquisition of the characteristics and norms of diverse cultures of which we are a part.

Yet, in some places, it appears as if God is a stranger. Why is God treated as such? Isn't He your Heavenly Father? Isn't He the One Who brought you out of the oubliette of darkness into His Castle of Light? Do you know God? Are you interested in connecting with Him? If so, I would like to encourage you to open your heart as you read on. I found God in my childhood days. You can find Him, too, if you haven't yet.

CONNECTING WITH GOD FROM CHILDHOOD

The story of my walk with God started from my childhood days. I understand that some people never had that opportunity, or they had it and did not have the chance to go deeper into spiritual realities. I would like to briefly share my story on how I encountered God.

I began to experience God's glory when I was a young child. I remember how my mom always took me to church and about my early yearning to go to Sunday school, where I had the opportunity to grow spiritually. In addition to being a geography teacher at our local secondary school, my mom served as a Sunday school instructor and a leader in the women's fellowship group.

I got to know God from a tender age. I beheld Him in His Word. I met other kids in church. And I was passionate about serving Him. Taking part in church activities was fun—attending Sunday services and youth group meetings, giving offerings, reading Bible verses in the main church, singing, drumming, and getting involved in performance art projects. I worshipped

God regularly in church. I prayed at home in my room as well. I really enjoyed studying the Bible.

Indeed, I was really inspired by an elder in my church that has gone on to be with the Lord. This man was so passionate about the things of God. He never wavered in his service to God. He was not a very rich man financially, but he was rich toward God.

In my walk with God, something remarkable happened. God revealed His Son, Jesus Christ, in an extraordinary way. There was an inner flame in me to serve God. During my teenage years, I steered off track at some point, but God put me back where I belonged. I just could not—and still can't—go away from Him. God will never allow that to happen because of His Light in my spirit.

I attended church services consistently. The Bible encourages people to go to church on a regular basis because it is important to gather together to worship God. Why wouldn't you want to worship the Person Who created you, the only One Who knows your end from the beginning?

WHERE DOES ONE CONNECT WITH GOD?

Some folks do not go to church. Others have stopped going to church for one reason or another. Some are vaulting from one church to another, looking for a place where they really feel they can belong. I understand that.

The experiences that some of you might have had in the church could have been contrary to what you expected. You might even have a tough perspective on the church. I understand that, too.

But did you know that Jesus Christ, the Son of God, is the Head of the Church? Jesus is your Lord and Savior. Throwing in the towel on Him is not the will of God.

There are some people who think they can be good Christians without going to church. The Christian Church has stood the test of time for over

2,018 years after Jesus Christ was resurrected from death and ascended to Heaven. As a young child of faith, I connected with God in the church and opened my heart to Him. I don't think it is worthwhile slamming the door on God.

I remember a few years ago when I was trying to introduce God to someone in my neighborhood.

"I believe God is in my heart; I don't need to go to church," he told me. "I watch different church programs on Sundays on television."

"This is good, but corporate worship is much more beneficial than solo worship," I told him.

After a while, in a dire situation, he eventually accepted my invitation to come to our church.

You could worship God anywhere—on the beach, in your home, in school, at work, in your car, or in a coffee bar. But Jesus encourages meetings of at least two people. When two or more people are gathered in the name of Jesus, He will be with them (Matt. 18:20). No matter how you worship God, gathering together in a church adds more value to your personal worship. God is thrilled with corporate worship.

You may be asking yourself, "Why should I go to church?" I have some answers for you.

The church is the bastion of light in a very dark world. Imagine what a world we would be living in if Christians did not pray. Anarchy would be rife. I spend some of my time praying for the entire world. For example, I spend time praying for the sick because I am touched by the feeling of their infirmities.

The church gives you an opportunity to walk in love. It is like a family; you get to meet other Christians and begin to share life with them. There is that sense of belonging. If you are struggling with an issue, the spiritual leader and the congregation can help you and pray for you as well. It's all about helping one another stay on track—my brother's or sister's keeper. You know what I mean, right?

The church gives you an opportunity to get a better perspective on God. I learned about God in church. You will get to understand God better when you go to church and listen to the Word of God being preached and taught. It also helps you know God profoundly through Bible study.

The church gives you an opportunity to grow spiritually. Your spiritual leader transmits spiritual information that blesses you and activates your faith. One of the ways God blesses you is through the words you receive from your spiritual leader. God gives different types of spiritual leaders to perfect His people—apostles, prophets, evangelists, pastors, and teachers (Eph. 4:11). These are all ministry gifts. Some ministers may have one or more of these ministry gifts. You spiritual leader is God's gift to you for spiritual nourishment.

The church is not just a place where people go to worship God. It represents who we are as the body of Christ. In Romans 12:5, the Church is called "one body in Christ." The Church is a family through which Jesus manifests Himself in the world today. As members of God's family, our salvation is secured (Jn. 10: 28-30).

The church gives you an opportunity to grow in the grace of Jesus Christ. Second Peter 3:18 instructs that you must grow in God's grace and His Word. Nobody in the church is perfect. God knows about that, for sure. No matter your situation, God's grace is sufficient for you (2 Cor. 12:9). His grace is always available, and it's your responsibility to take advantage of it, just as the apostle Paul admonished Timothy (2 Tim. 2:1).

BROKEN BUT STRONG

As the youngest child in a family of seven, I am thankful to God that I was raised early on with the gift of proximity to His Word through a blessed family. I believe God had a special plan and purpose for my life by placing me in that family.

Despite my family's inextricable closeness to God, my dad went through a protracted illness and passed on in December, 1994. During his period of sickness, Dad could barely talk, and he found it increasingly difficult to sit up straight or to eat. This was so devastating for my family. I was just nine years old when he finally passed, and I remember vividly going into my room and praying that God would raise him from the dead. I knew the story of how Jesus raised Lazarus from death in the Bible. I was praying to God, thinking He would intervene supernaturally. Was I chasing the wind?

Be it as it may, I had to carry my cross. What I mean here is that I had to endure a thorny situation. I knew everything has its time. I knew the darkness would vanish. I knew God's Light would outshine the darkness. The beauty of His Light eclipsed all the darkness. I thank God for His faithfulness. He gave me ample grace to heal. I have learned to always love and trust God—no matter the situation.

I don't know the context of your relationship with your parents. However, the Bible instructs us in Ephesians 6:2-3 to honor our parents, so that we may live a good life and live long on the earth. I have found the spirit to celebrate my parents privately and publicly. Learn to forgive your parents—love them, speak well of them, support them, provide for them, and always seek their wisdom.

THE PERCEPTION OF LIGHT AND DARKNESS

There is a spiritual component to light and darkness beyond the physical aspect. God is Light, and this is absolutely in contrast with darkness. How do light and darkness relate to your life? Simply speaking, light represents everything that is consistent with God's nature, character, and manifestation. Jesus used light to paint a picture of good works.

Darkness represents anything that is inconsistent with God's nature, character, and manifestation. For example, love is light, and hate is darkness.

Peace is light, and anger is darkness. Wisdom is light, and foolishness is darkness. Which do you honestly desire: light or darkness?

Light is one of the first things God established as recorded in Genesis 1:3. The Hebrew phrase *yehi 'or*[2] literally translated in the English language means "light, exist." This was a command from God calling into reality something that did not exist before. God spoke light into existence; light shone out of darkness.

In Second Corinthians 4:6, God's Light is further revealed in the context of liberating us from our unworthiness, weaknesses, and sinfulness through the knowledge of the glory of God in His beloved Son: "For God, who commanded the light to shine out of darkness, hath shined in our hearts, to give the light of the knowledge of the glory of God in the face of Jesus Christ."

"Light" is related to "luminary"—a source of light. When God created the world, He made two types of lights and the stars—"the greater light to rule the day, and the lesser light to rule the night" (Gen. 1:16). These lights were set in the heavenly realms to give light upon the earth. The greater light in this Scripture represents the sun, and the lesser light represents the moon. The sun rules by day, and the moon rules by night.

The sun, the moon, and the stars have different kinds of glory and differ in beauty and brilliance (1 Cor. 15:41). The sun's glory is very distinct compared to the moon and the stars.

The greater light (sun) is tremendously significant and splendid. Its glory exceeds all other heavenly bodies. The Hebrew term for "greater light" is *gadowl ma'owr*,[3] which means "great brightness," and "lesser light" is *qaton ma'owr*,[4] which means "a diminutive brightness." God referred to night as darkness in Genesis 1:5. The Bible frequently likens darkness to sin (Acts 26:18, Isa. 60:1-3). Consequently, anything that is not of light is darkness.

---

2 *Bible Hub, s.v.* "Yehi Or," Accessed January 3, 2018, http://biblehub.com/text/genesis/1-3.htm.

3 *Bible Hub, s.v.* "Gadowl Ma'owr," Accessed January 3, 2018, http://biblehub.com/lexicon/genesis/1-16.htm.

4 *Bible Hub, s.v.,* "Qaton Ma'owr," Accessed January 3, 2018, http://biblehub.com/lexicon/genesis/1-16.htm.

What is the darkness that you are experiencing in your life? What is that thing that you want to get rid of in your life that keeps bothering you?

Imagine you know a sixteen-year-old girl. She was a virgin, living in an area where there was a civil war. One night, terrorists took her and a bunch of other girls away. They were raped every day and made sex slaves. They were released after several years of captivity. The pain and shame haunted them for a very long time. This would be a mentally draining situation. This is absolute darkness!

Imagine you know a single mother with three kids from three different men. She is going through a lot. She just lost her oldest child; then she had a love affair with a new guy in the neighborhood and became pregnant for the fourth time. Frustrated with the whole scenario, she is thinking about aborting the baby. The guy beats her most of the time. She can't take it anymore. She is so confused that her head is almost spinning. Darkness is written all over her face.

Imagine you know a guy that has been with his employer for over a decade. Pay is great. He's all smiles. Suddenly, he receives the most dreaded phrase in the world—"You're fired." He didn't do anything wrong. He was just terminated for no good reason. He's now receiving unemployment benefits. But he's not sure about his next steps. He's been applying for jobs, but no employer has even called him for an interview. His days are becoming darker and darker. He's so frustrated that he goes into binge-drinking mode, hoping to find some solace. Then, drugs enter the scene. His girlfriend abandons him. He begins to contemplate suicide. The suicidal thoughts won't go away, but instead, they hammer him relentlessly. It keeps coming on and on. Suddenly, darkness has taken over his life.

Imagine you know a beautiful and smart lady. She graduated top of her class from a reputable university and landed a job as a sales manager in a successful company. She went on a business trip with her boss, the vice president of sales and marketing, to close a business deal. Bang, they clicked on all cylinders. They had dinner together at the hotel restaurant to celebrate. The appetizers, main courses, and desserts were fantastic. She didn't drink beer, liquor, or wine. She opted for some fresh apple juice. As the night went on, they chatted and giggled. She was pressed at some point and left for the washroom. By the time she came back, her boss had slipped drugs into her glass of apple juice. He took her to his hotel suite and sexually abused her. With all the shame, depression, and humiliation, she quit her job. Her life became clouded in darkness.

Imagine you know a hardworking guy. He's divorced with two kids. He never expected things were going to come to this. He is in pain but still loves his ex-wife. He reminisces about her from time to time. He is frustrated and confused with his life. He always travels about 180 miles back and forth once a month for three months to see her and the boys. He calls her and the boys about once a week. He hoped his former wife and he could remarry, but she has another lover. He feels like she's gone forever. It's like chasing the wind. His darkness won't go away.

Maybe you are in business, and everything has been all right. At some point, your customer base shrank, and cash flow plummeted. You can't get things going. You are putting in so much effort, and all you feel like is trash. Your customers owe you and are incapable of paying you. You are having a hard time generating new business. You feel tortured by low business performance. You are thinking of shutting down your business or declaring bankruptcy. The darkness is here!

ARE YOU FED UP WITH LIFE?

Are you feeling like you are fed up with life? Perhaps, all the excitement is gone. Do you feel like your dreams are not being fulfilled? Your soul is tormented. You are becoming livid. You believe things are not working in your favor. You wonder, "Why was I not born into some rich family?" You are sick and tired of not being excited about life.

You leave home for work, and you are mad for no reason. You are unhappy with yourself. You are stressed. You are becoming more bitter every day. It appears there's no one that can really help you.

The smiles have vanished. Your face looks frightening. You are secretly fighting with yourself every day. You are unable to unclutter your mind. Negative thoughts are piling up. You are afflicted with despair. Who can pull you out of all these dark places?

The answer is God. God is offering you a second, third, fourth, tenth, hundredth, or thousandth chance. He is full of mercy. Stop crying! You may not be able to get it all together, but God can.

I remember a lady who was diagnosed with cancer. Being a woman of faith, she trusted God in her battle. She came out strong and victorious. God restored her health. The pain and shame are all gone, and she is still serving God today, walking in the glory of His Light. The anointing of the Holy Spirit has given her the transcendent life—a supernatural life beyond the dictates of this world.

One of the ways you could get God to solve your problem is through the prayer of petition. I have implored God many times, and my petitions have always been granted. It is like an attorney bringing strong arguments before a judge in a court of law. You can reason with God. For example, I failed my road test twice before I got my driver's license. I was so mad that I took the case to God. We reasoned the matter out, and God ruled in my favor. When I went for the third road test, everything was all right.

God is more likely to grant your petition if you have been faithful, serving Him rightly. The extent of your service and faithfulness to God represents your body of evidence to query God in every situation that is unfavorable to you.

Job was a God-fearing and wealthy man (Job 1:1-3). The devil attacked him. He was afflicted with diseases and lost all his wealth. Darkness came upon him. Amid all the afflictions, he did not stagger in his faith in God. He never gave up. He kept his integrity. God rewarded him. His fortunes were twice as much as he had before. He was healed of all his diseases.

How can you move toward restoration? You can receive restoration by changing your thought patterns. You can't have a great relationship with God with an unstable mind—today you believe, tomorrow you don't. You must reset your mind. God wants you to transform your mind (Rom. 12:2). Can you really get a new mind? Yes. How? Through His Word. God's Word is Truth, and it makes you free (Jn. 8:32).

The most powerful tool you have at your disposal is your mind. Your mind is the home to memory, decision-making, discernment, and awareness. Your mind is a treasure, so protect it. Where do you think stress, worry, anger, rebellion, and low self-esteem come from? A dark mind. If God's Light floods your mind, do you know the difference it will make?

Can you imagine that your mind is a war zone? The enemy—that devil of darkness—will always try to attack your mind. If he beats you in your mind, the game is over. Renew your mind daily with God's Word (Rom. 12:2). Mediate and give yourself unto it (Josh. 1:8). As Proverbs 4:22 instructs, pay close attention to God's Word, and it will bring healing to your entire body.

No matter the situation you are going through, God's Light is a plausible solution. God's Word is Light. Light stands for truth. How can you function in the glory of God's Light? All darkness is made manifest by God's Light. God is the Father of Lights. Do you want to be a child of Light?

Jesus is the real Light. Malachi 4:2 describes Jesus as **"The Sun of righteousness . . . with healing in his wings."** You are God's child—a child of Light. In Ephesians 5:8, the apostle Paul encourages the church in Ephesus to "walk as children of light." Light reproduces light. Darkness reproduces darkness.

It is your responsibility to make your light shine—whether it is to two, three, or a million people. No wonder Jesus Christ declares in Matthew 5:16, **"Let your light so shine before men, that they may see your good works,**

and glorify your Father which is in heaven." As a child of God, you inherently possess His glory—a glory that overcomes every kind of darkness in humanity. You are part of this generation for a reason—to light up your world.

So, the million-dollar question is, what rules your life—light or darkness? How can you have light in your life?

Psalm 119:130 states, **"The entrance of thy words giveth light; it giveth understanding to the simple."** The focus in this Scripture is not God's Words but its entrance (entry, ingress, penetration). For example, when you read the Bible, which is Divinely inspired by God, the Light penetrates your spirit and produces Divine understanding or wisdom. In that process, God's Spirit would help you discern and comprehend His Word easily.

Since God's Word is light, why should you remain in darkness? In John 8:12b, Jesus declared, **"He that followeth me shall not walk in darkness, but shall have the light of life."** Maybe you've gotten to a stage in your life where you don't know what to do next. You are in a place of ambiguity and puzzlement. You are in a place of darkness. What are you going to do?

Imagine you had a great wintertime wedding with your partner. You are back from your honeymoon on the island of Maui. After a couple of weeks, you start feeling some pain. It begins to get worse, so you decide to go to the hospital. Your physician diagnoses you with terminal cancer. She informs you that you have six months to live. What can you do to overcome this nightmarish situation?

In the wake of the bad news, you and your spouse decide that you both should tour the world before you die. Visiting places around the world is great fun, right? You embark on a global expedition, starting from Vancouver to Las Vegas to Mexico City to Rio de Janeiro to Johannesburg to Brisbane to Bangkok to Dubai to Rome to Rabat to Puerto Rico and, finally, to New York City. You just want to live your best before you die. After all, life is too short and sometimes full of surprises. You reminisce how you were five years old, then ten years old, then twenty years old, then forty years old; and now, you are heading to the grave.

But what do you have to lose at this point? Everybody will die at some point in his or her life. When Jesus was on the earth, He demonstrated the power of God through the mighty miracles that He wrought. Miracles are real. Miracles still happen today. Sometimes, fear and doubt can easily accelerate people toward their graves because they have given up all hope. To receive Divine healing, you must have faith (Matt. 17:20).

God has given some amount of faith to every human being (Rom. 12:3). You build your faith by continually imbibing God's Word (Rom. 10:17). For example, Jesus healed a bleeding woman, who was in that condition for twelve years (Matt. 9:20-22). This woman had faith that she would be healed if she touched Jesus' garment. In a crowded scenario, she pushed through the crowd just to get to Jesus. When she touched His garment, the bleeding stopped immediately. Jesus told her she received healing because of her faith.

The good news is that you can turn around any hopeless situation. Focus on the Truth of God's Word. Cancer is a fact based on medical science. Divine health is reality based on God's Word. God's Word has the power to change facts to spiritual realities. This is because the spiritual realm has dominion over the physical realm. See yourself in the light of God's Word. God wants you to be healthy. If you are sick, I pray in the name of Jesus that you will live again and not die.

JESUS IS THE LIGHT OF THE WORLD

Jesus is the Light of the world. If you follow Him, there will be no darkness in your life. If you allow God's Word to come into your spirit, you will realize that the Light of God's Word will shine in your spirit. When you follow Jesus, you will find yourself living in the perfect will of God.

Darkness cannot stand the presence of light. As a child of God, you walk in God's Light. That is why the Bible reminds you of your Divine power: **"No weapon that is formed against thee shall prosper . . . " (Isa. 54:17).** God has bestowed His righteousness on His children. What this means is that you should not live in fear of anything because God is faithful to protect you and bless you with His victory.

WALKING IN THE GLORY OF GOD'S LIGHT

What does it mean to walk in the glory of God's Light? First, to walk in the glory of God's Light, you must be born-again. But many fear this term. For example, in church or during a Christian conference, the minister announces, "Are there any people here who would like to become born-again? What I mean is, would you like to accept Jesus Christ as your Lord and Savior?" Sometimes, people respond to the call; sometimes, they don't.

If you are in this kind of situation, you may be thinking that you don't want to abandon your way of life. But to truly follow Jesus Christ, there are some things that you must let go. You don't know if that was your last call to salvation.

There is a cemetery close to where I live. When I am driving by, I cry in my heart. Where did all those people go? Heaven or Hell?

To be born again, all you need to do is confess and accept Jesus Christ as your Lord and Savior. As written in Second Corinthians 5:17, when you become born again, God doesn't count your past life against you anymore because He has given you a new life. You've now become the righteousness of God (2 Cor. 5:21). Your physical body remains the same, but your spirit is recreated anew in Christ Jesus. The Holy Spirit illuminates your life and empowers you to live a new life based on God's Word. Your spirit eventually takes over your physical senses.

For example, imagine that you used to be a prostitute in a red-light district. You decided to start going to church. One of your former clients calls you. You feel the urge to hook up, but your spirit tells you to say no. There are conflicting thoughts in your mind, and you do not want to miss out on the big bucks. What you are faced with here is a temptation. The solution is God's Word.

Remember, Satan tempted Jesus three times after He was baptized (Matt. 4:1-11). Jesus used Scriptures to defeat Him. Temptations start in your mind. You can use Scriptures to counter any kind of temptation. God will guide you. Don't be afraid. You will not lose anything.

Second, to continually live in the glory of God's Light, you must have God's Word abiding in your recreated spirit. With God's Word embossed in your heart and mind, the glory of His Light cannot be turned off. It is a continuous manifestation of God's Word at work in your life. I have meditated so much on the Word that when I am in crisis, I don't need to rush to go read the Bible. There is a rich deposit of God's Word in my spirit that comes forth. For example, I might feel down, but God's Word says that I should **"rejoice always"** (1 Thess. 5:16). That simply activates the joy of the Lord in my spirit.

CONNECTING WITH GOD THROUGH YOUR SPIRIT

God loves you so much and wants to connect with you. However, you must first believe in Jesus Christ. In John 3:16, the Bible tells you how God loves the world and has given you an open invitation to believe and trust in Jesus Christ so that you will enjoy life on Earth and Heaven and not be a victim of spiritual death and after-death.

Connecting with God must be an everyday experience whereby you are **"filled with the Spirit; speaking . . . psalms and hymns, and spiritual songs . . . giving thanks always . . . unto God"** (Eph. 5:18b-20). Many people live in frustration because they are not continually filled with the Spirit. God has called us into a supernatural life. If you operate from a worldly perspective, the filling of the Spirit could be a herculean task. When you need to fellowship with God, I would encourage you to shut down the television, your smartphone, and other distracting devices and give God the attention that He deserves. It makes a huge difference.

Being filled with God's Spirit continuously activates an atmosphere of God's glory. But why is humanity still ravaged by sickness, disease, and death? These things result from spiritual death in the human body. The existences of these things have left many people perplexed.

Imagine a spiritual person being terminally ill. Why can a dying physician not save himself from a ruinous disease? Sickness and disease resulted from the fall of Adam and Eve, and through Satan. However, if God's Spirit that raised Jesus Christ from the dead abides in you, it would vitalize your mortal body (Rom. 8:11). The Bible says, **"Then shall thy light break forth as the morning,"** and you shall have health in your body (Isa. 58:8). **"Christ hath redeemed us from the curse of the law"** [which includes diseases and sicknesses] . . . (Gal. 3:13).

LIGHT IS RIGHTEOUSNESS

Light symbolizes righteousness. In Psalm 112:4, we see that no matter the darkness, our righteousness in God through Jesus Christ always thrives.

God has been gracious to us by revealing His Light (Psa. 118:27). Righteousness represents right-standing before God—a position whereby you are accepted by God without guilt.

In the Old Testament, God did call Israel to live in obedience to the Law. Israel fell short. Humanity has fallen short of God's glory (Rom 3:23). Both the Old Testament and New Testament teach that salvation and righteousness come through faith (Gen. 15:6; Num. 21:8-9; Hab. 2:4; Jn. 3:14-16; Gal. 3:17-22).

Jesus gave us His righteousness as a gift (Rom. 5:17). Therefore, you cannot be more righteous than me and vice versa. You have been saved—not because of your righteous deeds but because of God's mercy (Titus 3:5). God is so rich in mercy that even in your transgressions, He still loves you. He made salvation available to you in Jesus Christ by His grace. In Christ, there is no denunciation.

Christ has been made unto you **"wisdom, and righteousness, and sanctification, and redemption"** (1 Cor. 1:30). God's wisdom is far above secular, academic, and satanic wisdom. You have also been sanctified—set apart by God for His glory. And you have also been redeemed from all sin. So, you should not be concerned about the sins you committed, are committing, or will commit. I will tell you why. If you have a genuine relationship with God, there is a permanent purification mechanism of our sins because we are walking in the light of God (1 Jn. 1:7). You were predestined to be saved by God. God has called you and, in so doing, justified and glorified you (Rom. 8:30).

NEW LIGHT IN YOUR SPIRIT

Light also symbolizes newness in the recreated spirit—a new glory. It shows you the personality of a born-again Christian. **"Therefore, if any man be in Christ, he is a new creature: old things are passed away; behold all things are become new"** (2 Cor. 5:17). Old things typify the life you had before you became born-again. New things typify the Divine life you receive in your spirit after you become born-again. In other words, your spirit and God's Spirit become one.

Jesus is urging you to walk in the Light so that you can always stay ahead of darkness (Jn. 12:35). This means you must maintain a good relationship with God. In that process, God would help you to overcome evil situations if they arise. If you believe in Jesus, you are born of God, and anything that comes from God overcomes the world (1 Jn. 5:4). Your faith has given you the victory over that evil thought. Wow! You have got to be conscious of your triumph. Don't give room for the enemy to wreak mayhem in your life.

I have found so much joy ministering to the Lord. This is very important. God needs your attention! Therefore, I was inspired by God's Spirit to write an expression of praise at the beginning of each chapter.

In case you don't know anything about God's Spirit, I would love to explain that quickly. God the Father sits on the throne in Heaven. Jesus sits at His right hand. God does not leave His throne. Jesus left the earth many years ago when He ascended to Heaven. So, the only way you can experience God is through His Spirit. He is the One that makes the presence of God real to you. God's Spirit gives you the anointing—supernatural abilities (Acts 1:8).

With the Holy Spirit, you are sure of God's power in your life. Without God's Spirit, you are powerless, like a sheep among the wolves. God's Spirit is so gracious. By His power, you can live an enjoyable life—moving from glory to glory, from grace to grace, from success to success, and from victory to victory.

Growing up as a Christian, I became conscious of my true personality in Christ Jesus. I believed in God's Word with all my heart, all my soul, all my flesh, and all that is within me. I cannot trust anything else in this world other than God's Word. His Word never fails.

I discovered that I have been enthroned, that I am a joint-heir with Christ (Rom. 8:17), and that I am the seed of Abraham (Gal. 3:29). Therefore, God tells us in Hosea 4:6 that His "people are destroyed for lack of knowledge." Many people live in limitation and ignorance because they have chosen to reject the veracity of God's Word.

GOD IS LIGHT; SO ARE HIS CHILDREN

Did you know as God's child, you are magnificent? **"But ye are a chosen generation, a royal priesthood, an holy nation, a peculiar people . . . "** (1 Pet. 2:9).

You live in Zion. You are a king and priest (Rev. 5:10). You are royalty, my friend. Don't settle for less. Jesus Christ is the solid Rock on which you stand.

You cannot fail when Jesus is the Lord of your life. If you fail, it means God has failed; and God never fails. He is an awesome God.

In Matthew 5:14, Jesus describes God's children as the "light of the world." This is so delightful. A true Christian will always shine wherever they go. God's children carry His presence. No wonder Jesus says, **"Let your light so shine before men, that they may see your good works, and glorify your Father which is in heaven"** (Matt. 5:16).

So, what is your job as a Christian? Your job as a Christian is to demonstrate the character of Jesus Christ and manifest the fruits of the Holy Spirit to the world because Jesus said, **"Ye are the light of the world"** (Matt. 5:14). You found your purpose in life—to sow seeds of the Good News. It will produce good fruit in those who accept the message of the Gospel. This is the Good News you are reading. I am sure you are getting blessed as you read on. Your life will never be the same again.

WHO IS RESPONSIBLE FOR THE DARKNESS IN THE WORLD?

There is someone responsible for the darkness in the world—"the devil," also known as "the evil one." Jesus calls the devil **"the prince of this world"** in John 12:31. This does not mean he is the owner of the world. He is simply a negative influence in the world. God remains the Supreme Owner and Ruler of Heaven and Earth (Psa. 24:1). The enemy controls the world through distorted ideologies, deceptions, and evil machinations. He is on a mission to demolish anybody. Why on earth would someone choose to connect with someone who is on a mission to devour you?

In the Bible, we see that God anointed Jesus of Nazareth with power; He performed many good works and healed people who were oppressed by the devil (Acts 10:38). For instance, Jesus fed five thousand people with five loaves of bread and two fishes (Matt. 14:13-21). Jesus also healed a disabled man at the pool of Bethesda who had been in that condition for thirty-eight years (Jn. 5:1-18). Jesus was always moved with compassion.

It is startling that some people trust medical science more than God's Word. For instance, your physician may diagnose you with a specific disease. That is just information. It is not the end of the world. What does God's Word say about you? The Holy Spirit is superior to the devil of darkness (1 Jn. 4:4). If you are sick, God says He will bring health back into your life (Jer. 30:17). Aren't you excited about this?

In your walk with God, you must ensure to walk continually in the light and not revert to darkness (Lk. 11:35). It is your responsibility to ensure that the life you live is consistent with God's Light.

Don't go back to your old ways. Thank God always, and pray that you don't fall into temptation. Become cognizant of your righteousness, and don't let sin overshadow you.

In Job 18:5 we see how **"the light of the wicked shall be put out, and the spark of his fire shall not shine."** The light of the wicked is the lesser light. Ecclesiastes 2:13 confirms that **"light excelleth darkness"** in the way **"wisdom excelleth folly."** Ecclesiastes 11:7 says, **"Truly the light is sweet . . . "** How beautiful it is to walk in the glory of God's Light—His manifest beauty and holiness. Light always triumphs over darkness.

Jesus is the Light of the world. **"I am the light of the world: he that followeth me shall not walk in darkness, but shall have the light of life"** (Jn. 8:12).

As a human being, you can perceive light from the sun or from an electric bulb with your physical eyes, but Jesus is not referring to that kind of light. What Jesus meant is that He is the Truth. Walk in the Light of His Word.

Believing in the Light gives you an opportunity to become a child of God (Jn. 12:36). The Lord wants you to be a light to those with whom you are in contact. He wants you to tell the Gospel (Good News) to them.

Three of Jesus' disciples—Peter, James, and John—had a direct experience of the glory of God's Light. In the transfiguration of Jesus in Matthew seventeen, Jesus took them up to the mountain to pray. Whilst they were praying, Jesus' facial appearance swiftly changed. His personal appearance and clothing were transformed into a glorified state—as white as light. Peter, James, and John, in a way hitherto they had never fathomed, reveled in the glorification of Jesus as the Anointed One—the King of kings and Lord of lords.

FROM DARKNESS TO LIGHT

There are many instances in the Bible where God has turned people from darkness to light. For instance, Saul of Tarsus (later the apostle Paul) was a man who perpetrated darkness. He had been stalwartly persecuting Christians—going from house to house putting them in prison. As a witness, Saul had agreed to the stoning to death of Stephen, who was a deacon at the early church in Jerusalem.

As seen in Acts 9:3-19 (NKJV), Saul was on his way to Damascus when he encountered Jesus.

> . . . **Suddenly a light shone around him from heaven. Then he fell to the ground, and heard a voice saying to him, "Saul, Saul, why are you persecuting Me?" And he said, "Who are You, Lord?" Then the Lord said, "I am Jesus, whom you are persecuting. It *is* hard for you to kick against the goads." So, he, trembling and astonished, said, "Lord, what do You want me to do?" Then the Lord *said* to him, "Arise and go into the city, and you will be told what you must do." And the men who journeyed with him stood speechless, hearing a voice but seeing no one. Then Saul arose from the ground, and when his eyes were opened he saw no one. But they led him by the hand and brought *him* into Damascus. And he was three days without sight, and neither ate nor drank. Now there was a certain disciple at Damascus named Ananias; and to him the Lord said in a vision, "Ananias." And he said, "Here I am, Lord." So the Lord said to him, "Arise and go to the street called Straight, and inquire at the house of Judas for *one***

called Saul of Tarsus, for behold, he is praying. And in a vision he has seen a man named Ananias coming in and putting *his* hand on him, so that he might receive his sight." Then Ananias answered, "Lord, I have heard from many about this man, how much harm he has done to Your saints in Jerusalem. And here he has authority from the chief priests to bind all who call on Your name." But the Lord said to him, "Go, for he is a chosen vessel of Mine to bear My name before Gentiles, kings, and the children of Israel. For I will show him how many things he must suffer for My name's sake." And Ananias went his way and entered the house; and laying his hands on him he said, "Brother Saul, the Lord Jesus, who appeared to you on the road as you came, has sent me that you may receive your sight and be filled with the Holy Spirit." Immediately there fell from his eyes *something* like scales, and he received his sight at once; and he arose and was baptized. So when he had received food, he was strengthened. Then Saul spent some days with the disciples at Damascus.

The things Saul did were horrible. This was someone who was persecuting Christians, intent on destroying the fledgling church. But the Lord, so rich in mercy, was very gracious to give him another chance.

You might have been involved in things that are unrighteous. But that does not mean you should linger in pain, shame, and regret. You can't change what happened in the past, but you do have control of what happens in your future. No matter how evil or wicked you are, the Light of God has the power to transform your life, so that you can become a child of light and of the day (1 Thess. 5:5).

THE REWARD OF WALKING IN THE LIGHT

One of the rewards that you will receive for walking in the glory of God's light is Heaven. Heaven is a place beyond the universe—a place without struggle, disease, or death; a place where God lives, as many people would fathom it. Believe me, Heaven is infinitely more beautiful than the best places you have visited.

The apostle Paul explicitly referred to the glory of the **"third heaven"** (2 Cor. 12:1-4). The third heaven is where you will find the highest level of God's glory. It is the abode of God, His angels, and spirits (saints who had been living in the world). God, the Father of Lights, sits on the throne of His Kingdom. God's **"glory [is] above the heavens"** (Psa. 113:4).

Your true home is beyond the skies—in Heaven. Sometimes, when I'm alone, I spend time meditating on the realities of God's Kingdom. What would it be like when we all get to Heaven? Did you know that God is preparing greater mansions for his faithful servants in the third Heaven? Can you imagine mansions built with gold, silver, beautiful gems, and stones? In John 14:2 (NKJV), Jesus said, **"In my Father's house are many mansions; if *it* were not *so*, I would have told you. I go to prepare a place for you."**

Don't spend your time here on Earth trying to build worldly treasures, which are vanities. The day will come when all these things will cease to exist (1 Pet. 4:7). Life on Earth means nothing except for the purpose of our Lord, Jesus Christ. Focus on storing your treasures (rewards) in Heaven, which is everlasting.

WHERE DID DARKNESS COME FROM?

The world is fraught with tremendous darkness—hatred, jealousy, envy, satanic oppression, corruption, drug addiction, terrorism, greed, war, genocide, homicides, child abuse, and suicides. When you turn on the television, it is just an avalanche of bad news. What is going on?

To understand how evil started, you must go back to the period after God had created the world. Genesis 6:5 (NKJV) states **" . . . that the wickedness of man *was* great in the earth, and *that* every intent of the thoughts of his heart *was* only evil continually."**

When Adam and Eve sinned in the Garden of Eden, humanity plunged into darkness. Humans became spiritually unglued from God. However, Jesus Christ, the **"last Adam,"** gave us a new life (1 Cor. 15:45). He brought us out of spiritual death and made us alive unto God.

Because of the Adamic inheritance of the sin character, human beings receive that nature from birth. But God does not condemn us for our sins. He is rich in mercy and lovingkindness, reconciling the world unto Himself, not counting our sins against us (2 Cor. 5:19).

God, through His Son, Jesus Christ, has already saved the world. When I look at people on the streets, especially on Sunday mornings, all I see is the image of God in them. This reminds me of Jesus' invitation to Simon Peter and Andrew in Matthew 4:18-20 to follow Him. Jesus wanted to make them **"fishers of men."** We've been called to make disciples of all nations (Matt. 28:18-20). Our primary job on Earth is to get people saved by the Gospel of Jesus Christ.

HAVE YOU EVER REJECTED GOD? TELL ME WHY.

Connecting with God brings light to your life. Let's imagine you don't know God and don't want anything to do with Him. You have never read the Bible, or you don't read it regularly. You are pursuing your career and pleasures. You are very successful. Then I meet you on the street, and I try to start a conversation about God.

Then you tell me right off the bat, "I'm not interested."

I respond, "Just give me a minute to explain something to you."

You say, "Go ahead."

Then I began to tell you about God's plan for your life. What is God's plan for you? God's plan for you is that you should be saved and that you should **"come unto the knowledge of the truth"** (1 Tim. 2:4). His plan is to reconcile you unto Him. He wants to have a great relationship with you. You feel like saying no, but something inside you is compelling you to open your heart to the message.

Then you begin to wonder why you reject God. Maybe you think you're too smart for God. Then I tell you, "Despite the good some people try to do, they might not make it to Heaven."

Romans 3:23 states that you have fallen short of God's glory. Adam brought spiritual death to humanity, but Jesus (the Last Adam) is a **"life-giving spirit"** (1 Cor. 15:45 NKJV). Jesus came into this world so that you might have life and have it plentifully (Jn. 10:10b). Isn't this new life a glorious promise? Something began to happen—you connected with God through the light of His glorious Gospel.

Jesus Christ died, was buried, and rose from the dead for your sake. He died for a purpose—to redeem you from all iniquity. He has given you salvation as a gift. It is free to everyone in the world. All you need to do is to believe in your heart that God raised Jesus Christ from the dead and to confess with your mouth that Jesus is your personal Lord and Savior, and you shall be saved (Rom. 10:9). Salvation is freedom from spiritual death and the afterdeath. God's gift to you is eternal life through Jesus Christ (Rom. 6:23b). If you are interested in receiving salvation, there is a prayer for you at the end of this book. I would like to encourage you to say the prayer when you get to that point.

Have you ever hurt someone in your lifetime—determinedly or unknowingly? Sometimes, you might find yourself doing iniquitous things, having wrong thoughts, or saying heinous words. Despite this hullabaloo in your spirit, God still loves you. God sent Jesus to the earth for you—not to condemn you, but to save you from all unrighteousness. Yes, I mean *all* unrighteousness. He lived, died, and was resurrected from the dead so that you would receive newness of life (Rom. 6:4). In the name of Jesus, I pray that the Lord purifies your heart by His Word and His Spirit. Then the totality of His beauty will shine in and through you.

ARE YOU IN A DARK PLACE?

Have you found yourself in a dark place, where you are uncertain of what is going to happen the next day? The psalmist vividly paints a picture of chaos and violence, which is akin to what is happening in our world: **" . . . the dark places of the earth are full of the habitations of cruelty"** (Psa. 74:20).

Only God's light can enlighten a dark place. Only God's light can rescue humanity. God wants to show you His Light today. This is an opportunity to get to know the Lord. He accepts you for who you are and not what people think about you. He created you in His own image. Did you know that He loved you first? He really loves you. He loves you the same way that He loves me.

Has the deceiver of the world shackled you in spiritual darkness? The devil operates through spiritual wickedness, principalities, and his rulers of darkness (Eph. 6:12). The enemy, the architect of darkness, has blinded the minds of millions of people around the world:

> **But even if our gospel is [in some sense] hidden [behind a veil], it is hidden [only] to those who are perishing; among them the god of this world [Satan] has blinded the minds of the unbelieving to prevent them from seeing the illuminating light of the gospel of the glory of Christ, who is the image of God** (2 Cor. 4:3-4 AMP).

It could be flustering to those seeking God to understand the nuts and bolts of spiritual warfare and spiritual blindness. But God is here to protect you from being entrapped by the enemy. The reason why many people are not interested in knowing God is because their spiritual eyes are closed. God wants to open your spiritual eyes.

God is the only One Who turns darkness into light. Are you looking to change things in your life? Let me introduce you to God, the **"Wonderful Counselor"** (Isa. 9:6). God is supernatural—beyond your natural senses. He knows the way out of darkness. Are you are looking for a miracle today or wondering if you might need one tomorrow? Stay glued to God. You will see the difference that it makes.

One day, I was feeling down. I don't know why. I was not feeling happy. Sometimes, it just happens, and you feel the urge to withdraw and stay on your own. I took my Bible and meditated on Scripture and prayed. The light of God's Word eclipsed the darkness. My experience has been that in my weakest moments, I rely on God and the light of His Word as my source of strength.

THE NEW HOLY CITY

In Revelation twenty-one, John describes how the first Heaven and the first earth will disappear. The seas will be gone. And he recounts the beauty of the holy city descending from God—New Jerusalem. God, Who created the world, will make all things new.

In the realm of the Spirit, John beheld this great holy city descending with the glory of God. It had the glory of God. The glory of the Light he saw was so great, like a pellucid and exquisite jasper stone. The glory of God lit the New Jerusalem, so there was no need for the light from the sun and the moon. It will be glory without nights.

One of the major benefits of having a good relationship with God is that your name will be found in the Book of Life—the Lamb's Book of Life (Rev. 21:27). To have your name written in this book, you must be considered righteous by God. If your name is not found in the Book of Life, the result will be the lake of fire and brimstone—a place of eternal torment and suffering (Rev. 20:10). Life is short. It is worthwhile to have a good relationship with God.

RECOGNIZING GOD'S GLORY

Has someone ever offered you a Bible for free? When I was a child, I received a free New Testament Bible from Gideons International. I was excited. I read the Bible like I had never done in my life. If you give a Bible to some people today, they would likely say, "I am not religious" or "I don't believe in the Bible."

I have encountered some people who had a hard time recognizing that they need to receive God's salvation. Part of the reason is that the enemy has blinded their eyes of understanding (2 Cor. 4:4). To believe God, you must hear His Word because you can't believe in something that you have not heard. There must be a strong connection between your spirit and God's Word.

God revealed Himself in His dear Son, Jesus Christ, while He was on the earth. Yet, many people in His day rejected Him. God, through Jesus Christ, came to the earth to live with us. He blessed kids, helped women, healed the sick, gave people food to eat, and so much more. Instead of being served, He served the people. He showed empathy for people's weaknesses. Some were not cognizant of His glory. Others received Him, beheld His glory, were born of God, and became God's children.

> **In the beginning was the Word, and the Word was with God, and the Word was God. The same was in the beginning with God. All things were made by him; and without him was not anything made that was made. In him was life; and the life was the light of men. And the light shineth in darkness; and the darkness comprehended it not. There was a man sent from God, whose name was John. The same came for a witness, to bear witness of the Light, that all men through him might believe. He was not that Light, but was sent to bear witness of that Light. That was the true Light, which lighteth every man that cometh into the world. He was in the world, and the world was made by him, and the world knew him not. He came unto his own, and his own received him not. But as many as received him, to them gave he power to become the sons of God, even to them that believe on his name: Which were born, not of blood, nor of the will of the flesh, nor of the will of man, but of God. And the Word was made flesh, and dwelt among us, (and we beheld his glory, the glory as of the only begotten of the Father,) full of grace and truth** (Jn. 1:1-14).

If you tell a toddler to say or do something, they usually obey. For example, if you tell the child to say "daddy" or "mommy," they will normally utter what you told them to say. If you tell them to stand up or sit down, they just do it. If you tell them to read a book along with you, they will go ahead and read. If you tell them to sing, they will sing. But if you give the same instruction to an adult, they will try to figure out the rationale of why you are asking them to do that.

To really connect with God, you must behave like a child. Kids are open-hearted. If you think you're too smart for Him, that makes it very difficult to see His glory. This is the God Who gave you everything that you have because He has already blessed you with all spiritual blessings in heavenly places (Eph. 1:3).

The moment you shut the doors to your spirit, it becomes very hard to know God. Some people don't even want to hear anything that has to do with God or Jesus Christ. Before my teenage years, I opened my heart to God's glory. I saw His glory in the Word being preached in church. I saw His glory in the Word that I read in the Bible.

SCRIPTURE REFLECTIONS (NKJV)
WITH BRIEF COMMENTARIES

Isaiah 5:20: "Woe to those who call evil good, and good evil; Who put darkness for light, and light for darkness; Who put bitter for sweet, and sweet for bitter!"

The Bible is very clear about what is good and what is evil. You cannot mix light with darkness. You cannot make a sweet thing bitter and a bitter thing sweet. Light is good, and anything inconsistent with light is darkness or evil.

Luke 1:79: "To give light to those who sit in darkness and the shadow of death, To guide our feet into the way of peace."

God wants to bring His light into your life. His light translates people out of darkness and gives them His peace.

John 3:20: "For everyone practicing evil hates the light and does not come to the light, lest his deeds should be exposed."

Evil is inconsistent with God's nature. Simply, it is unrighteousness. Evil people hate the Light. God's light has the capacity to expose those things which are inconsistent with His nature, character, and manifestation.

John 12:36: "'While you have the light, believe in the light, that you may become sons of light.' These things Jesus spoke, and departed, and was hidden from them."

Jesus is the Light. Believe in Him. He is the Light because He shines the spotlight on our sin and clearly enlightens the path for our redemption.

Acts 26:23: "That the Christ would suffer, that He would be the first to rise from the dead, and would proclaim light to the Jewish people and to the Gentiles."

Jesus rose from the dead and lives in Heaven with His Father. He has proclaimed the Truth in the light of God's Word to both the Jews and non-Jews (the Gentiles).

1 John 2:9: "He who says he is in the light, and hates his brother, is in darkness until now."

> *Light is love. You can't say you are walking in love if you can't love those in your home, school, workplace, or neighborhood. Hurting others around you is not love. You'll be walking in darkness unless you decide to consciously love others.*

Revelation 22:5: "There shall be no night there: They need no lamp nor light of the sun, for the Lord God gives them light. And they shall reign forever and ever."

> *In this new realm, in the beauty of holiness, God's glorious Light will shine forever. There will be no such thing as night or daylight from the sun.*

PRAYER

Father, in the name of Jesus, I glorify You because You are the Light. No darkness shall operate in my life because I have been translated out of darkness into the glory of Your awe-inspiring Light. I pray that Your Light floods my spiritual eyes so that I will love You and see how all things work together for my benefit. Your Light shines in me, from glory to glory. Your beauty, grace, and righteousness are manifested in my life every day. I am blessed. Amen.

2

THE GLORY OF GOD'S LOVE

Father, Thou first loved me.

Thy Love is unconditional.

Thy Love is amazing.

Thy Love is sweeter than honey.

Thy Love is tastier than wine.

Thou lovest me, O Lord.

O Lord, I lovest Thee, too,

With my all my heart,

With all my soul,

With all my strength.

Thy steadfast love endureth forever.

Thy love is impeccable.

Thy love casteth all trepidation.

Thy love heals me.

Thy love never fails.

Because of your love,

All detestation is gone.

The Bible tells us two things about God's nature: **"God is love"** (1 Jn. 4:8), and God is also a Giver (Jn. 3:16). He gave you His only Son, Jesus Christ, to redeem you from all your iniquities and usher you into the realm of eternal life. Growing up, I found John 3:16 to be one of my favorite Scriptures. It is embossed in my heart.

Someone told me a couple of months ago that he was having suicidal thoughts. He told me, "The devil is playing with my mind." I reminded him that God loves him. I told him about John 3:16, that because he believes in Jesus Christ, he would have everlasting life and not perish.

Having suicidal thoughts is a fact. But God's saving Word should be your real experience—it gives life. I told him to continually meditate on God's Word in the Bible, pray frequently, and ensure he attends church services on a regular basis. The solution is replacing the suicidal thoughts with spiritual activities.

GOD LOVES YOU MORE THAN YOU CAN EVER IMAGINE

The world has been engulfed in sin since the fall of Adam and Eve in the Garden of Eden. Today, sin has become more wicked. It is no surprise. It appears the level of evil is skyrocketing, and more seems to be on the way, like a tsunami.

However, God still reaches out to us, when **"we were yet sinners"** (Rom. 5:8). God loves even those who don't believe in Him. However, I want you to be conscious of God's righteousness because Jesus Christ has given that to you.

When I was living in Swansea, Wales, I met a lady who told me, "There is no God."

I replied, "There is a living God."

"How can I believe in a God that I cannot see or feel?" she asked me.

"God is real, and He is in Heaven with Jesus Christ, His beloved Son," I said. "God manifests Himself in the world today through the Holy Spirit."

Finally, she began to understand that people can connect with God through His Spirit. The Holy Spirit is the conveyor of God's presence. He comes from the Father (Jn. 15:26). He is the One Who makes God real to you.

He is the Voice of God. He brings the Word of God to you. Without the Holy Spirit, it would be challenging for you to know God intimately.

REACHING OUT TO UNBELIEVERS IS AN ACT OF LOVE

Reaching out to unbelievers is an act of immense love. Many times, I have encouraged people to consider connecting with God. My obligation as a Christian is to reach out to the world. I do it because I love God and people. I just want to have a conversation with people I meet. I encourage other Christians to do likewise—whether through writing, music, teaching, preaching, or participating in evangelism projects. In recent years, I have been involved in evangelism initiatives in Quebec, Canada. I do this because I love the Lord, and I love the people. It is genuinely excruciating to see people just reject God's Word right off the bat. However, we must keep doing the work of ministry until Jesus Christ comes again.

FOCUS ON GOD'S LOVE

No matter how challenging the situation is that you find yourself in, I would like to tell that you that it is not over yet. You might be depressed, thinking of committing suicide, or be in some very bad situation. Stop worrying! Stop saying, "What if?" Stop thinking that things might get worse. Worry sets up a magnetic force that attracts negativity into your life. Worry helps make your fears possible.

Change your focus, and meditate on God's love. God has shed His love in your heart by the Holy Spirit that dwells in you (Rom. 5:5). God's love has been poured into your spirit. As you reflect on God's love, all fear dissipates.

God has graced you with His goodness. Bless the Lord with all your soul and with all that is within you. Right now, you are winning **"because greater is he that is in you, than he that is in the world"** (1 Jn. 4:4b).

LOVE GOD AND EVERYONE ELSE

The two greatest commandments in the Bible focus on the theme of love. Matthew 22:37-39 (NKJV) says, **" '. . . You shall love the Lord your God with all your heart, with all your soul, and with all your mind.'** This is *the* first and great commandment. And *the* second *is* like it: **'You shall love your neighbor as yourself.'"**

Loving God means worshipping Him **"in spirit and in truth"** (Jn. 4:24) and fellowshipping with Him. If you love God, you will adore Him and do what He asks you to do. The term "neighbor" refers to anybody in the world—your family members, your friends, your sisters and brothers in the church, people you don't know, and the world at large. If you are vacationing in Paris and you meet a panhandler on the street, that's your neighbor. If you are visiting New York City and you see a heartbroken girl on the street, that's your neighbor. If you are visiting London and you see someone stranded at the airport, that's your neighbor.

Always be open to expressing love, just like the Good Samaritan in the Bible (Lk. 10:25-37). In this story, a Jewish traveler was stripped of his clothing, beaten, and left on the road in a near-death situation. First, a priest came by, and then a Levite. Both of them ignored the injured man. Finally, a Samaritan stopped. Even though Samaritans and Jews hated each other, the Samaritan helped the man. What an act of love!

In 2012, a fellow brother in Christ and I met a lady at a grocery store in Montreal, Canada. She looked troubled.

"Are you, all right?" I asked.

She hesitated to utter a word, but then, suddenly, she opened up. She told us about her refugee situation. We told her we were Christians, and we came around the grocery store to tell people about God. Eventually, we led her to Christ. She was so gleeful that she accepted our invitation to come to church.

In 2016, I met two teenage girls at a metro station in Montreal, Canada. When I saw them, I called to them, and they walked over to meet me. After chatting with both of them, I realized that they did not know God. I asked them if they wanted to know God and receive Jesus Christ as their Lord and Savior. They said yes. I prayed the prayer of salvation with them, and they were born again. They were excited to receive God in their lives. There are many teens out there that need help and direction. Between the ages of twelve and seventeen is a very crucial time in anyone's life. Knowing God at that stage helps.

Love is the quintessence of life. You can do all the good things in this life; but without love, you are lacking something momentous. If you genuinely demonstrate love, it will be difficult to sin. Among the intrinsic forces of faith, hope, and love that endure, the greatest of these is love (1 Cor. 13:13). Let love prevail in your life.

WHAT IS LOVE?

I believe you have some knowledge of what love is all about. But how does the Bible define love? First Corinthians 13:4-13 (NKJV) sheds more light on the subject exquisitely:

> **Love suffers long *and* is kind; love does not envy; love does not parade itself, is not puffed up; does not behave rudely, does not seek its own, is not provoked, thinks no evil; does not rejoice in iniquity, but rejoices in the truth; bears all things, believes all things, hopes all things, endures all things. Love never fails. But whether *there are* prophecies, they will fail; whether *there are* tongues, they will cease; whether *there is* knowledge, it will vanish away. For we know in part and we prophesy in part. But when that which is perfect has come, then that which is in part will be done away. When I was a child, I spoke as a child, I understood as a child, I thought as a child; but when I became a man, I put away childish things. For now we see in a mirror, dimly, but then face to face. Now I know in part, but then I shall know just as I also am known. And now abide faith, hope, love, these three; but the greatest of these *is* love.**

Isn't this amazing? The apostle Paul presents the greatness of love. Can you love like this? Prophecies, tongues, and knowledge cannot compare to the power of love. A couple that I know recently got divorced. When I heard the news, I cried deeply in my soul. The question I would like to ask you is, how far or how deep is your love?

Our spirits yearn for love. Our spirits can love. In my experience, I have yet to see someone who doesn't like being loved. Something is broken inside a person who does not appreciate being loved.

Love conquers everything. Love prevails in every circumstance. Without love, you are living in darkness. Without love, you are bound to be envious of others, proud, ruthless, sinful, unfaithful to God, hopeless, and impatient.

Then, what is perfect love? Perfect love is when you love God with all your heart, and you know that He loves you unconditionally. There is no fear in the realm of perfect love. If you know this secret, your life will never be the same again.

Perfect love emanates from Jesus. Jesus loves you and gave up Himself for you (Gal. 2:20). What a sacrifice! He is the Lamb of God. When you accept salvation from Him and walk in righteousness, wisdom, sanctification, and redemption, you reciprocate perfect love.

There are a plethora of fears in the world. It could be in your relationships, in the workplace, and in the direction in which our society is headed. If only you knew and experienced God's perfect love, you will never live in darkness.

THE LOVE OF MONEY

One of the things that could derail us from our walk with God is the love of money. Can you love God and money at the same time? The Bible tells you that you cannot love God and money at the same time (Matt. 6:24). What does this mean?

With money, you can do whatever you want. From a worldly economic perspective, it is legal tender. From a biblical perspective, money is a "seed."

It appears some people worship money and see no need to worship God. You might be thinking, "I have a beautiful mansion, nice cars, and money in the bank. I don't need God." It is understandable that we live in a material world where money is important, but the love of it will lead you to sin. Why do some people trust money more than God?

The Bible says it is easier for a camel to go through the eye of a needle than for a rich man to make it into God's kingdom (Matt. 19:24). If you find yourself in a position where money has become more important than God, then money has become an idol to you. What would you do if you didn't have money?

The idolization of money poisons the mind with fretfulness and worries. Some people have obtained wealth through oppression, avarice, fraud, covetousness, and sin. God warns the rich to trust in Him and not in unsure riches (1 Tim. 6:9-17; Jas. 5:1-5; and Lk. 12:16-31). Remember life is more than food, and the body is more than clothing and material possessions.

GIVING TO GOD IS A SACRIFICE OF LOVE

Giving is a privilege that God has bestowed upon us. One of the ways we demonstrate our love for God is through our giving. To some people, this might sound controversial. But I will show you why giving is an important spiritual principle.

In 2009, I visited a rural village in Africa. Most of the people there were farmers. I was happy that they had a local church in the community where I could go and worship God. One certain Sunday, I visited the local church. They were having a thanksgiving service. I was amazed at how they loved and worshipped God with their crop harvests and monetary offerings. Despite their poverty, they were rich toward God because they gave cheerfully.

In First Kings six, we see how King Solomon of Israel built the house of the Lord. Solomon was a very wealthy and wise king who succeeded his father, King David. He was also considered a prophet who really loved God. In his fourth year of reign, Solomon started building the temple and finished it in his eleventh year. It was a magnificent temple. Solomon is widely praised for building God's temple. He worshipped God with his wealth.

In the Christmas story, the magi (wise men) traveled all the way from the East to offer gifts to the baby Jesus (Matt. 2:1-12). They acknowledged the greatness of the newborn King. This was a great act of love. They worshipped the Lord with their wealth.

If you love someone, wouldn't you happily offer that person a gift? We offer gifts during Christmas. But where is Jesus' gift? Giving to God is an act of love. It must be done joyfully. Offerings are not meant to enrich your spiritual leader. In the quest for accountability, some people end up criticizing the church because of an apparent cornucopia of wealth. The church is part of the body of Christ and needs to be governed with adequate resources. Offerings given in church are used for the work of the ministry. Jesus is coming again, and His expectation is one of a glorious church—a church that flourishes with resources.

If you are not a believer, the topic of giving might sound strange to you. The reason I am discussing giving and love is that it's in the Bible and is part of the Christian life. Giving to God must be based on your means and how much God has blessed you (Deut. 16:17). God urges you that at the end of every week, you should lay something aside for Him, so that you may prosper (1 Cor. 16:2). You must give God your best because you have been called to a life of giving. Proverbs 3:9 (NKJV) says **"Honor the Lord with your possessions, And with the first fruits of all your increase."** Your attitude matters in giving. The Bible says that God loves a cheerful giver (2 Cor. 9:7). Giving is an expression of our love toward God.

Let me tell you a short story about a business mogul who loved God. This man was so generous. He understood the principle that giving to God was a demonstration of his love for Him. He gave to God cheerfully and was never broke. His business empire never crumbled. God blessed him enormously. He gave great sums of money for church construction projects. He knew God loved him, and he reciprocated God's love by getting involved in church projects. He never wavered in his giving. He knew that the more he gave to God, the more financial and spiritual blessings he would receive.

You have the power to receive a hundredfold increase from God (Mk. 10:29-31). I remember the great recession back in 2008 that plagued the global economy. If we were to have another global economic meltdown, what would you do? Would you be rattled by news headlines on economic limbo, budget deficits, volatile stock markets, debt crises, unemployment, negative consumer confidence, inflation, and tax hikes? This rich man never bothered himself with any such news because his prosperity was not dependent on the news media or the state of the economy. As a giver to God, he operated from a different set of principles because he was part of the kingdom of Heaven.

God is eternal. But what can we give to God—the Owner of Heaven and Earth? He is **"the same yesterday, and today, and forever"** (Heb. 13:8). Humans can never out-give God. Whether you give God one dollar or one billion dollars, you will be blessed as a measure of what you really have.

In Luke 21:1-4, a poor widow placed two mites into the church treasury whilst the rich folks were also giving. Jesus noted that she gave the best because that was all she had. God is more interested in our attitude in giving than the amount. If it is the last penny or dollar bill that you must give, God will certainly reward you for that because His Word says, **"It is more blessed to give than to receive"** (Acts 20:35b). The blessing is for the one who gives.

Giving, as an act of love, should not be limited to the four walls of the church. It spans beyond that. Besides giving to God through your local church (financially, spiritually, and physically), you are also called to give to the poor. In the summer of 2018, I met a distressed woman in downtown Montreal. She was in need of money. Through the move of God's Spirit, I went to a nearby ATM and gave her some money. Apart from the fact that when I give to the poor, I am lending to God, I also know that God has blessed me, and I am His ambassador on the earth. I know that I have to bless those in my world, especially the poor. Never hesitate to give to the poor. When you help the poor, you are lending to God, and He will pay you back.

There was a certain man named Zacchaeus in the Bible (Lk. 19:1-10). He was the chief tax collector in the city of Jericho. The people did not like the man because they viewed him as crooked and conspiratorial. Zacchaeus heard Jesus was coming to town. Because he was a short man, he decided to climb a sycamore tree so that he could see Jesus. When Jesus noticed him in the tree, He said that He would pay him a visit at his home. Zacchaeus pledged half of his money to the poor and said he would pay back those he had cheated four times the amount. Jesus said to him, **"Today salvation has come to this house, because he also is a son of Abraham; for the Son of Man has come to seek and to save that which was lost"** (Lk. 19:9-10).

Farmers sow seeds to receive a harvest. A sown seed needs water to grow. After growth comes harvest time. In this light, the things that you do daily can be likened to seeds. Ensure the things you do bless other people. You can't be negative and expect nice things to come your way. You reap what you sow (Gal. 6:7).

For example, when you plant generosity you reap generosity. When you plant love, you reap love. When you plant kindness, you reap kindness. I remember a time when I provided sublime service to a customer, and she gave me a decent tip, which reflected the level of services I provided her. She reciprocated my professionalism and kindness in a spectacular way. In Genesis 8:22, God declares that there is seed time and harvest time. It will never stop. It is a spiritual law.

HEALTHY AND PROSPEROUS

In Third John two, the apostle John prayed for his beloved friend Gaius to be healthy and prosperous as his soul also prospers. Gaius walked in faith, love, and truth. If you would love to serve God but are stifled by financial woes, I would like to share with you five things that you must do to function in financial freedom:

First, you must reduce and eliminate debt as much as possible. Financial burdens are dangerous. The root cause of debt is one's attitude to spending. Every project has a cost. Don't spend unless you know you have the capacity to pay for your expenses (Lk. 14:28). Any type of credit has a cost. Repay your debts as much as you can—mortgage, personal loans, student loans, car loans, credit lines, and credit cards.

Second, you must manage your money responsibly (Prov. 21:20). Focus on your needs and not your wants. If you earn $2,000 a month, having a monthly car payment of $750 is not a good idea. Make sure you keep money aside for savings and long-term investments. And the Bible encourages us to care for our relatives (1 Tim. 5:8). Help your family members, especially those who are not as financially buoyant as you are.

Third, you must honor God with your giving (Prov. 3:9-10). You give to bring glory to God. God is the One who supplies all our needs. He has already blessed us with all spiritual blessings in Heavenly places (Eph. 1:3). He has also given us all things that pertain to life and godliness (2 Pet. 1:3).

Fourth, you must trust in God (Jer. 17:7-8). Our lives can be transformed when we put our trust in God. There might be some turmoil going on in your life. In John 15:5, Jesus says we can do nothing without Him. Trusting God and not yourself to guide and lead you is the right thing to do (Prov. 3:5-6). You must trust God, in good times and in bad times. In my life, I have avoided many bad decisions because I trusted Him.

Fifth, you must shun greed for money. In 1 Timothy 6:10-11, Hebrews 13:5, and Luke 12:15, people are encouraged not to idolize money. **"No man can serve two masters: for either he will hate the one, and love the other; or**

else he will hold to the one, and despise the other. Ye cannot serve God and mammon" (Matt. 6:24). Put God first in everything. The Bible encourages us to put our focus on serving God and His righteousness, and He will give us all the things that we need (Matt. 6:33).

THE DIMENSION OF LOVE

Do you really understand the dimensions of God's love—the length, breadth, and depth of His love? My beloved brothers and sisters, why do we have so much vitriol and covetousness in our world today? Why have some devoted their lives to earthly security and comfort for themselves and their families? Is this really what life is all about?

Genuine Christianity is the demonstration of the character and virtues of Jesus Christ. Before His death, Jesus was oppressed, afflicted, and tortured, but didn't fight back. He was like a silent lamb being led to slaughter. Jesus died for the world. This is the greatest demonstration of love. He was rich; and for your sake, He became poor so that you might be rich (2 Cor. 8:9). One thing I have learned from Jesus Christ is humility.

Let us look at His life for a moment. Jesus Christ loved the world—the world of sinners. He washed our sins away with His blood—a costly sacrifice. Jesus Christ loves you, and He wants you to express kindness, compassion, and forgiveness to other people as He did when He walked the face of the earth. Learn to be a blessing to others.

WALKING IN THE GLORY OF GOD'S LOVE

Walking in the glory of God's love is not that arduous. You can start today if you have not already done so.

First: Do things to others, as you would expect them to do unto you (Lk. 6:31). For example, I simply don't belittle people for any reason because I won't appreciate being belittled. I remember an incident when someone talked down to me, and I decided not to retaliate. I just ignored the situation as if it never happened.

Second: Love your enemies because God will reward you for it (Lk. 6:35). In one of my jobs, my boss suddenly became furious with me for making an operational error. This was an issue that could easily be rectified. She even threatened to take the matter to human resources and get me fired. Instead of taking her anger personally, I promised that I would not make the same mistake again and then prayed about the situation, and the storm was over.

Third: Shun evil ways and desire to sincerely love people (Rom. 12:9). I remember a woman who mistakenly left about $1500 in an envelope inside the post office where people fill out forms. The envelope was just lying unnoticed for a while. When I got there, I saw the envelope, opened it, and was startled to see it contained a great deal of money. I could have easily just put the envelope in my pocket and walked away. It was about two weeks before my wedding. I had to travel from Montreal, Canada, to Swansea, United Kingdom, for my wedding, so I could have been tempted to keep the money. While I was planning to take the envelope to the post office manager, the lady came to me and asked me if I had seen an envelope with money. I said yes and returned the $1500 to her. She was very thankful and rejoiced greatly.

Fourth: Protect, trust, hope, and persevere in love (1 Cor. 13:4-8). Don't walk away from your spouse or partner. It is painful to see couples divorced or separated. This is not God's plan. I understand that it can be a tough situation. In my marriage, my wife and I have been able to protect each other, trust, hope, and persevere in good and bad times. It is so very important that you protect those whom you truly love. Don't let the other person walk away from the relationship. Ask for forgiveness, or forgive the other person if you need to. Sometimes, you must beat down your big ego. It is as simple as that.

I remember a story about a couple who were involved in a messy situation. They used to fight and slammed each other frequently. The couple eventually divorced, and the level of abhorrence spiraled out of control after disconnection. They both have new spouses, but the hate is still there. This is too much negative energy that could make your head spin. Wouldn't it be fantastic if they were to forgive each other?

Fifth: Love all the time (Prov. 17:17). Be consistent in your love for God and others. There have been times in my life that I seriously felt like questioning God for the things that I was going through. I learned a long time ago to endure hardship because our light afflictions are just for a moment (2 Cor. 4:17).

Oh, dear Lord Jesus, when I look in the rearview mirror and think of Your love for me and how I love You, I have no other option but to walk in the light of Your Love. Thank You, Jesus, for loving me so dearly.

There was a time in my life when it was so difficult for me to get a job. I said to myself because Christ lives in me, things will change. Eventually, I found a new job.

Thank You for never forsaking me. I love You, Lord!

Sixth: Realize that God is Love (1 Jn. 4:8). You are not a non-entity, with no one who cares about you. You may not know God, but He knows everything about you. Get to know Him, so that you can know how to love. God is the quintessence of love. He is the Father you have been looking for all your life. The best way you can get to know and love God is through fellowship with His Word.

Seventh: Love God, and serve Him. Our purpose here on Earth is to love and serve God all our lives. Leave everything else aside. Set your gaze on God, the Father of Lights. In Matthew 6:33, Jesus commands you to seek the Kingdom of God first before anything else. By doing this, all other things that you need will be made available to you. This is the right order of affairs, not the other way around. We should always put God first. Anything else can come after that—family, career, business, personal finances, houses, cars, investments, and so much more.

In Matthew 19:16-30, a rich young ruler came to Jesus to inquire about the things he needed to receive eternal life. Jesus told him to sell all his possessions and give the proceeds to the poor—for he would receive treasure in Heaven. Jesus also said that he should follow Him after doing this, but the young man did not want to give up his wealth, so he walked away sorrowfully. Are you able to do this?

Matthew 5:3 says, **"Blessed are the poor in spirit: for theirs is the kingdom of heaven."** Being 'poor in spirit' means that you give up your material possessions for spiritual humility. Jesus gave the rich man a spiritual instruction, and he was unable to trust and obey the Master. Therefore, he could not receive any Heavenly blessing.

Eighth: Hold fast to His love. No situation can separate you from God's love—tribulation, distress, persecution, famine, nakedness, peril, or sword (Rom. 8:35). Hold on to His love no matter what is happening in your life. God will always be there for you.

I remember a distressful situation I went through a couple of years ago. I was stranded when I first arrived as a postgraduate student at Swansea University. I did not have a place to stay for that night. I had called to make arrangements for my school accommodation, but the arrangements had not been finalized. I met a "good Samaritan" guy in front of the school library. He convinced his friend to help me stay at his place for a few days. After that period, I signed a lease with a landlord not very far from where I was temporarily staying. It was amazing how God turned people's hearts to love me in a distressful situation. I am grateful that God sent someone to help me.

Ninth: Be humble as you walk in the light of God's love. God expects you to be humble because He has a great plan to promote you. There is a story about a man named Joseph in the Bible (Gen. 39). His brothers sold him as a slave to the Ishmeelites, who then sold him to the Egyptians. Joseph worked as a slave for an Egyptian official named Potiphar. Potiphar's wife was infatuated with Joseph. She wanted him to sleep with her, but Joseph refused to commit adultery. She took revenge and accused Joseph of attempted rape. Potiphar charged Joseph with rape and put him in prison. Years later, Pharaoh then had dreams that only Joseph could interpret. After interpreting the dreams, Joseph was appointed prime minister of Egypt by Pharaoh. Because of Joseph's humility, he received a tremendous promotion.

To walk in love in any area of your life, you must demonstrate humility. Arrogance and pride can really stifle your progress in life. Are you thinking you are better than you really are? First Peter 5:5-7 instructs:

. . . Yea, all of you be subject one to another, and be clothed with humility: for God resisteth the proud, and giveth grace to the humble. Humble yourselves therefore under the mighty hand of God, that he may exalt you in due time: Casting all your care upon him; for he careth for you.

Humility pays!

Tenth: Decide to love. It is not that difficult. You can make good decisions, and one good decision you can make is to love. I have decided to love everybody and not withhold love from anyone, especially those in the body of Christ. You can do likewise. There might be one thing that is stopping you from loving, which is fear. But I can guarantee you that God's love casts out all fear (1 Jn. 4:18). Love is one of the fruits of the recreated human spirit (Gal. 5:22-23). Decide not to withhold love from others because you have love in your spirit. Try it! It works!

GOD LOVES YOU SO VERY MUCH

Did you know that God's love for you is precious and never fails (Psa. 36:7)? I cannot count the number of times that God has lavished His love, grace, and mercy on me. In 2012, in Montreal, Canada, I could have drowned in the waters and died. The company I was working for at that time decided to take all the employees out for a boat ride. Everyone was out there swimming when I began to drown. One of my colleagues spotted me and came to my rescue. I believe God miraculously used him to save my life.

In 2017, on the Toronto-Montreal Highway 401, I could have been involved in a deadly car accident with my family. I was driving at about sixty miles per hour. A passenger car that was in the emergency lane was trying to merge into my lane. It appeared there would be a collision. In a split second, I found out that I was able to move to the left lane to prevent the collision in the right lane. My wife was shocked at what happened as she was sitting in the front passenger seat, and my son was behind her buckled in his car seat.

In both instances, I felt God's presence immediately, and the storm was over in the twinkling of an eye. These are testimonies of God's Divine protection. Without God's intervention, you would not be reading this book today. As God's child, I was given a Divine life, covered under His protection. I know in my spirit that I dwell in God's most secret place, that He is my Refuge, and that He delivers me from all evil (Psa. 91). The evil day came, but I was at peace knowing that He is with me.

THE VALUE OF LOVE

Love has tremendous spiritual value (1 Jn. 4:20). Love can solve a multitude of problems. The devil likes to turn people against one another—husband versus wife, parent versus child, employee versus boss, and even nation versus nation. Sometimes, people might do things that you do not like, but confronting someone to the extent of engaging in a physical battle is not worth it.

For example, when a driver illegally passes me, I just laugh. Why waste my precious energy on road rage? Your real enemy is the enemy who plants resentful thoughts in other people's minds. When those people act against you, you feel like they are your nemesis. When I notice someone is acting against me, I will simply rebuke the spirit that is causing that person to act that way.

EXPRESSIONS OF LOVE

How can you show that you love God? You can demonstrate your love for God by loving Him with all your heart, soul, and mind (Matt. 22:37). For example, I demonstrate my love for God through my talents. I wrote this book because I love God, and I love you, too. The extent of your love for God will determine the extent of your spiritual growth. The apostle Paul noted that "all things work together for good to them that love God" (Rom. 8:28). The more you love Him, the more you will mature in spiritual things, and the less you will care about the things of the world. As a Christian, you can't say you love God and hate other Christians because if you can't love those that you see, how can you love God that you have not seen? (Lk. 10:25-28).

LOVE IS RECIPROCAL

Did you know that love is reciprocal? It's not a one-sided show, with one person receiving all the love and giving nothing in return. In John 14:15, Jesus Christ says that He expects you to reciprocate His love by obeying His commandments.

There is so much that could change your life if you would love God and others. Allow God's love to flow through you. When His love begins to work in your life, you will find out that loving others isn't that difficult.

Sometimes, people get sick and die because of bitterness and hatred. Life is too short and too precious to allow that to happen to you. Please, show some love to your family, your friends, your neighbors, your colleagues, and even those whom you don't like as well. God has deposited love in your spirit. If He did not do that, He would not tell you to love Him or love others.

SCRIPTURE REFLECTIONS (NKJV)
WITH BRIEF COMMENTARIES

Psalm 119:127: "Therefore I love Your commandments more than gold, yes, than fine gold!"

This is King David talking about how God's Word is more valuable to him than fine gold. He puts God first. God's Word is so precious.

Proverbs 12:1: "Whoever loves instruction loves knowledge, But he who hates correction *is* stupid."

Loving God means doing what He asks you to do. God's Word is a sure guide for your life.

2 Corinthians 9:7: *"So let* each one *give* as he purposes in his heart, not grudgingly or of necessity; for God loves a cheerful giver."

Some people hold back when it comes to worshipping God with their substance. When you offer money to God, give what your heart tells you to. This pleases God. He loves those that give joyously.

2 Corinthians 13:14: "The grace of the Lord Jesus Christ, and the love of God, and the communion of the Holy Spirit *be* with you all. Amen."

Paul prays for the Corinthian church that they would walk in God's love, grace, and fellowship.

Ephesians 5:2: "And walk in love, as Christ also has loved us and given Himself for us, an offering and a sacrifice to God for a sweet-smelling aroma."

You should always walk in love because Jesus Christ loves you.

Ephesians 5:28: "So husbands ought to love their own wives as their own bodies; he who loves his wife loves himself."

For the married men, you and your wife are one. If you love yourself, that should translate into loving your wife.

2 Thessalonians 3:5: "Now may the Lord direct your hearts into the love of God and into the patience of Christ."

The apostle Paul is praying for Christians in the church in Thessalonica, that God will cause them to walk in love and patience—two important virtues of a Christian.

PRAYER

Father in the name of Jesus, I thank You for Your love, grace, and mercy. I love You, Lord, because You love me unconditionally. I will walk in the light, as Jesus is in the light, and I have fellowship with Him as His blood cleanses me from all sin. I receive the fullness of God's love. My love is perfected in Him, O Lord. I pray that from this day on, I will express more love for my neighbors, bosses, colleagues, family members, friends, enemies, and my country. In the name of Jesus. Amen.

3

THE GLORY OF GOD'S WORD

Bless Thee, O Lord,

From Word to Flesh,

From Flesh to Heaven,

From Heaven to Earth,

From Earth to Heaven.

Thy Word is a citadel.

Thy Word is life.

Thy Word is virtuous.

Thy Word is hallowed.

Thy Word is light.

Thou art the Word,

The living Word,

The filling Word,

The leading Word,

The compelling Word.

O Lord, Thy Word saves;

Thy Word abides;

Thy Word is wisdom;

Thy Word engineers;

Thy Word is timeless.

Now the Spirit expressly says that in latter times some will depart from the faith, giving heed to deceiving spirits and doctrines of demons, speaking lies in hypocrisy, having their own conscience seared with a hot iron, forbidding to marry, and commanding to abstain from foods which God created to be received with thanksgiving by those who believe and know the truth. For every creature of God *is* good, and nothing is to be refused if it is received with thanksgiving; for it is sanctified by the word of God and prayer. If you instruct the brethren in these things, you will be a good minister of Jesus Christ, nourished in the words of faith and of the good doctrine, which you have carefully followed. But reject profane and old wives' fables, and exercise yourself toward godliness. For bodily exercise profits a little, but godliness is profitable for all things, having promise of the life that now is and of that which is to come. This *is* a faithful saying and worthy of all acceptance. For to this *end* we both labor and suffer reproach, because we trust in the living God, who is *the* Savior of all men, especially of those who believe. These things command and teach. Let no one despise your youth, but be an example to the believers in word, in conduct, in love, in spirit, in faith, in purity. Till I come, give attention to reading, to exhortation, to doctrine. Do not neglect the gift that is in you, which was given to you by prophecy with the laying on of the hands of the eldership. Meditate on these things; give yourself entirely to them, that your progress may be evident to all. Take heed to yourself and to the doctrine. Continue in them, for in doing this you will save both yourself and those who hear you (1 Tim. 4 NKJV).

God showed me these words a couple of years ago. It is a clear instruction from God to be a good minister of Jesus Christ. It is my job as God's servant to nourish you with words of faith and good doctrine that I have followed since my childhood days. My expectation is to be a good example to believers and unbelievers through the word, love, faith, and holiness, and to demonstrate exemplary spiritual leadership until Jesus Christ comes again. It is worthwhile to reveal to you the realities of eternal verities—to help you to walk in love, righteousness, and grace.

WHAT IS GOING ON IN THE WORLD?

With all that is happening in the world today, many people have no clue what the future holds for them. Look at the terrorist attacks, natural disasters, wars, famine, refugee crisis, economic hardship, and human suffering. The thoughts of the second coming of Jesus Christ should give us hope. We should be sober, continuing to pray for the world. God is our hiding place— our refuge. Death is the chief of terrors, but Jesus is our Shepherd and has overcome death.

The occurrences of recent cataclysmic events are well documented in the book of Revelation. We are living in the last days. In 1 Peter 4:7, the Bible informs us that the end of the world is coming soon, with an exhortation to be alert and disciplined for prayer. This means that Jesus is coming again. Are you ready? The Rapture will happen soon when all Christians—living and resurrected dead—will be caught up with Jesus to join Him in eternity. The Rapture will set the stage for the Great Tribulation, during which the Antichrist will appear.

In these last days, you must hold on to God's Word more than ever before. The ministry of the Holy Spirit will help you navigate through life successfully. God expects your life to be a manifestation of His Word. Therefore, the Bible declares that Christians are **"the epistle[s] of Christ"** (2 Cor. 3:3). Remember that the Holy Spirit is the One Who empowers you. You should be very careful about the kinds of doctrines that you subscribe to in these last days. If a doctrine is not consistent with God's Word, then it is darkness. Reject it immediately!

God said that Heaven and Earth shall vanish, but His words would not (Matt. 24:35). There will be a time when the earth will disappear, and we will have a new Earth. The land and sea will be gone. There will be a complete change. In Revelation 21:1, the apostle John confirms this: **"And I saw a new heaven and a new earth: for the first heaven and the first earth were passed away; and there was no more sea."**

God's Word is eternal—yesterday, today, and forever. Why would you believe in anything other than God's Word? The world was created by God's Word. His Word lives on forevermore.

God's Word is a training guide that tells you how to live a successful life. He gave you His Word to live by. The mystery of Christianity had been hidden for a long time, and now has been revealed in Colossians 1:27b: **"Christ in you, the hope of glory."**

Christianity is the life of God (the Anointing) at work in a human being. "Christ" means the "Anointed One" or Christos"[5] in Greek (Lk. 4:16-19). The life that He has is the same life that He gives to those who follow Him. Christ (the Anointing) in you is a revelation that you must embrace. Jesus Christ didn't come to the world to bring a new religion. Back in His days, the religious folks were the ones that orchestrated His death. Jesus Christ was God made flesh. Since He left the earth, He gave us His Spirit to abide in us.

TAKEN AWAY FROM THE WORD

One of the ways the devil distracts Christians is by taking them away from the Word. He knows the power of the Word. He does not worry about those who don't read the Bible. If you are a Christian who can't find an hour in your day to fellowship with God through His Word, don't you think something is amiss?

Many Christians struggle in life because they don't spend enough time meditating on God's Word. Why should you struggle in life when you have

---

5 *Bible Hub, s.v.* "Christos," Accessed July 5, 2018, http://biblehub.com/greek/5547.htm.

God's Word available to you in the Bible? Perhaps you could start today by spending fifteen minutes meditating on God's Word and praying as well.

The accurate knowledge or discernment or recognition (Greek: *epignó-sis6*) of God's Word is paramount for your spiritual development. You must make sure that what you hear in church is consistent with God's Word. I always verify teachings with Scripture. God's Word is replete with power. God's Word is infallible, impregnable, and everlasting. If we live by God's Word, we demonstrate our faith in Jesus Christ.

What if God is calling you to serve Him? What if He wants you to serve Him before you retire? Or are you waiting to serve Him when you retire? Do you plan to play catch-up after a youthful experience of chasing vanities? It might be too late. Take advantage of the opportunity to serve God. Desire godliness. Your body is the temple of God. So, don't pollute it with sinful deeds. This is a virtuous caveat.

Did you know sin is insurgence against God? Romans 6:23 reveals that sin leads to spiritual death. I beseech you by the compassion of God that you come to the Father, as a child would gravitate toward their parents. God is interested in seeing your name in the Book of Life (Rev. 3:5). If your name is not found in this Book, you will experience the second death in the Lake of Fire—eternal punishment—ceaseless agony.

ARE YOU STILL DISAPPOINTED?

Many people have been languishing in depression, sickness, and pain for so long that they tend to utter expressions such as, "I'm sick and tired of . . . "; "Same old . . . "; "That's the way life is"; "What else can I do?"; and "I can't take it anymore." It is not surprising to see people in such conditions over a very long period. Why should anyone suffer in life for too long? If you are suffering right now, decide to connect with God and get out of your mess. You can't keep being a victim in life.

---

6 *Bible Hub, s.v.* "Epignósis," Accessed July 5, 2018, http://biblehub.com/greek/1922.htm.

You can get rid of your past and current malaise. Focus on your future by walking in the light of God's Word. It is not God's plan to see you perish (2 Pet. 3:9). He wants you to know the Truth and be saved (1 Tim. 2:4). The prayer of salvation at the end of the book gives you a great opportunity to repent and receive the gift of salvation.

THE BENEFITS OF GOD'S WORD

God's Word is very beneficial to you. It sustains you. Meditating on God's Word brings life and good health to you (Prov. 4:20-22). The Word of God has healing power. And it is good medicine.

How do you feel when you don't eat anything for an entire day? Your stomach would complain, "I need some food in here." In like manner, God's Word is spiritual food. If you avoid it, you will be deficient in spiritual nourishment. God's Word is food for your soul and spirit.

God's Word gives life. Everything about life is in God's Word. **"For they are life unto those that find them, and health to all their flesh"** (Prov. 4:22). If you find yourself in a tough situation (you are unable to pay your mortgage or rent), search the Scriptures and speak the "rhema"7 (the specific Scripture that addresses the situation).

To deal with the situation, you can speak out Philippians 4:6, which says, **"Be careful for nothing; but in every thing by prayer and supplication with thanksgiving let your requests be made known unto God."** Then you can pray like this, "Father in the name of Jesus, I glorify you for your peace in my life. Lord, I receive the money that I need because you always supply my needs. I glorify you for your blessing. Amen!" This is how I would use the rhema of Philippians 4:6 to deal with the situation.

Perhaps you have been inflicted with a health issue, or you know someone who is seriously ill. God anointed Jesus Christ with the Holy Spirit, and He went

---

7 *Bible Hub, s.v.* "Rhema," accessed January 3, 2018, http://biblehub.com/greek/4487.htm

about healing those who were oppressed by the devil. The curse of sin is the cause of illness. If you are oppressed in your body, it is not God Who did that. God is the One Who has the healing power. He loves you so much that He wants to help you. He wants to bring healing to you through His Word. Embrace Him with your faith. As described in Acts 20:32, I commit you to God and the Word of His Grace so that your life will be built in the right way. If you give yourself to the ministry of the Word, I guarantee you that there will be a change in your life.

APOSTLE PAUL MINISTERS THE WORD

In Acts 17, we read about the apostle Paul, who was in the Greek city of Thessalonica, which had a strong Jewish community. For three consecutive Sabbaths, he preached to them from the Scriptures on the resurrection of Jesus Christ. Some of the people bought into the Good News and joined the ranks of Paul and Silas—among them many God-fearing Greeks and aristocratic women. But other Jews were frantic and acrimonious over the conversions and organized a mob to crack down on Paul and Silas.

Moreover, they broke into the house of Jason—a Jewish convert and early Christian believer—accusing him of hiding Paul and Silas. They mocked Jesus and hailed Caeser. So, Jason and his friends had to pay a lot of money to be granted bail while city leaders investigated the charges. Paul and Silas escaped in the night with the help of their friends and went to Berea, where they met with another Jewish community.

They were treated much better in Berea than Thessalonica. The Berean people received God's Word gleefully, and it stirred faith in their spirits. They met with Paul daily and studied the Scriptures to see if Paul was accurately telling them the truth. Most of them believed, including influential men and women.

When the people in Thessalonica heard what had happened, they wasted no time in organizing a mob in Berea to crush Paul and Silas. Paul escaped to Athens, while Silas and Timothy stayed behind.

In Athens, Paul waited for Silas and Timothy, who were still in Berea. Athens was a junkyard of idols, and the people were crueler. Paul talked about this with the Jews and like-minded people at their meeting place. He even got to know some Epicurean and Stoic cognoscenti. Some of them dismissed him with sarcasm.

However, others that listened became more interested in the Good News. Paul then took the open space in Areopagus and declared the Word boldly.

> **It is plain to see that you Athenians take your religion seriously. When I arrived here the other day, I was fascinated with all the shrines I came across. And then I found one inscribed, TO THE GOD NOBODY KNOWS. I'm here to introduce you to this God so you can worship intelligently, know who you're dealing with** (Acts 17:22-23 MSG).

Paul critiqued the Greek idol-worship and preached on God's greatness, omnipotence, and omnipresence. God created the world and all its creatures, including human beings. He made the earth inhabitable for humanity. He admonished that God was calling for repentance and would judge the world on a set day. He told them that the Judge, Jesus Christ, had been raised from the dead.

When they heard the phrase "raised from the dead," the listeners were divided: some derided him, and others said they wanted to hear more. Others who were persuaded then and there stuck with Paul, among them Dionysius the Areopagite and a woman named Damaris. This is how the people treat God's Word today. Some buy into it and are blessed, while others perish because they reject the Word.

The resurrection of Jesus is the foundation of Christianity. Jesus Christ is the firstborn of the dead (Rev. 1:4). Jesus Christ is **"the resurrection and the life"** (Jn. 11:25). The resurrection of Jesus is God's gift to humanity. God gave us a new life (2 Cor. 5:17), His Divine nature (2 Pet. 1:4), and freedom from sin (Rom. 6:13).

THE WORD FLOURISHED IN THE CITY OF EPHESUS

God's Word is power. It is dynamic in nature with miracle-working abilities. Ephesus was a secular and booming city. In Acts 18 and 19, we see how Paul taught in the synagogue at Ephesus for three months. Paul also taught in the school of Tyrannus for about two years. The Gospel spread throughout Asia (a Roman province), and many people received salvation. Many of the new converts abandoned their pagan lives and burned their magician books worth fifty thousand pieces of silver. Paul left for Macedonia and instructed his protégé Timothy to stay in Ephesus to continue ministering the Word.

Ephesus is no different than what we experience in our world today. People frown at anything Christian-related, such as the person who told me straight to my face, "I don't believe in God or the Bible. I don't believe in anything." However, the Good News is still flourishing today, changing hearts and transforming lives through the glorious proclamation of the Gospel and the demonstration of the power of God.

In a parallel soul-winning account in the Bible, the apostle Peter preached God's Word, and three thousand people received salvation and got baptized (Acts 2:41). Later, the number of believers increased to five thousand.

GUIDED BY THE WORD

Life is filled with choices. God's Word helps you to make the right choices. Your present life reflects the choices you made in the past. You need proper guidance as to how to go about your life. Your body of knowledge has its limitations. But God's Word is the true Light (Jn. 1:9). Psalm 119:105 corroborates this: **"Thy word is a lamp unto my feet, and a light unto my path."** God's Word can provide good counsel, especially when you must make tough decisions. In times when you are in a dilemma, God's Word gives you the solution that you need.

> **For the word of God is quick, and powerful, and sharper than any twoedged sword, piercing even to the dividing asunder of soul and spirit, and of the joints and marrow, and is a discerner of the thoughts and intents of the heart. Neither is there any creature that is not manifest in his sight: but all things are naked and opened unto the eyes of him with whom we have to do** (Heb. 4:12).

This means that there is no subject matter that is not within the confines of the Word. The Word of God is Truth (Jn. 17:17). Seeing with the true Light means looking at everything from the dimension of God's Word. How do you perceive things around your life? If your decisions are not based on the Word, then I can guarantee you that you are on the wrong track.

In Colossians 3:16, Paul teaches that you can have rich deposits of God's Word in your spirit. Practice making God's Word your focus. In John 14:15, Jesus says if you love Him, you should keep His Word.

Remember that you must grow in the Word. Don't assume you know enough. Second Peter 3:18 says, **"But grow in grace, and in the knowledge of our Lord and Saviour Jesus Christ . . . "** When I continually study the Scriptures, Jesus Christ reveals Himself to me from glory to glory.

God's Word is Spirit and Life. It can uphold you in all dimensions. When the devil tempted Jesus and asked Him to command stones to turn into bread if He is truly God's Son, Jesus replied, **" . . . Man shall not live by bread alone, but by every word that proceedeth out of the mouth of God"** (Matt. 4:4). This is truly a glorious statement. The essence of life is God's Word. The devil could not comprehend it. It shattered him. So, if you want to live a triumphant life, you must live according to the authority of God's Word. God's Word illuminates your life. Through His Word, the darkness in your life is dispelled.

God's Word is inextricable from God. God's Word is your underpinning. It is your foundation. It has the power to build you up and give you an inheritance among the saints (Acts 20:32). You can encourage yourself in the Word. When you do, it gives you the ability to transcend all your challenges.

King David of Israel was troubled and distressed, as recorded in 1 Samuel 30:6. His people talked about stoning him. Faced with a dire situation, he had to encourage himself in prayer, casting the situation before God. It does not matter what you are going through right now. You can encourage yourself in God's Word, combined with prayer, and you will find the operative power to change any situation.

WHAT DOES IT MEAN TO SPEAK IN TONGUES?

Speaking in tongues, also known as *glossolalia*,[8] derived from the Greek ase glōssais lalein[9], which means speaking in a language unknown to you, is one of the ways you can be strengthened in God. In Acts two, we see how the followers of Jesus received the Holy Spirit and spoke in several languages.

The question you might be asking is, "Why do some Christians pray in other tongues?" Let me answer this. Before you pray to God, He already knows the intents of your heart. There are no words from you that are holy enough to express the highest form of worship to Him. *Glossolalia* does not go through the mind. It comes straight from your spirit. It is the flawless form of prayer that is sanctified by the Holy Spirit.

In 1 Corinthians 14:15, the apostle Paul said he **"will pray with the spirit, and . . . with the understanding also."** Paul gave primacy to praying in other tongues first. It is a spiritual language that God understands. Maybe you don't know how to pray in tongues. Maybe in your church, they don't pray like that.

Let me share this with you. In the church I attended when I was growing up, they did not pray in tongues. There was another church close to where I

---

8 Colman, Andrew, *A Dictionary of Psychology* (Oxford: University Press, 2009), https://books. google.ca/books?id=UDnvBQAAQBAJ&printsec=frontcover&dq=Andrew+M.+Colman&h l=en&sa=X&ved=0ahUKEwjh8fv8hfLcAhWOTN8KHeMGBnUQ6AEIKjAA#v=onepage&q= Andrew%20M.%20Colman&f=false

9 *Bible Hub*, s.v. "Glōssais Lalein," accessed January 3, 2018, http://biblehub.com/ greek/1100.htm.

lived. The Christians there prayed in tongues. I was curious, because I knew there was some power in the kind of prayer they were engaging in.

One day, I was studying the Bible, while lying on my bed, and I began to pray in other tongues. I was led by God's Spirit to start praying in tongues. It was an awesome experience.

When I find myself in a wearisome situation, I instantaneously start praying in tongues. My spirit is stirred up, and the Holy Spirit makes a speedy intervention. When I was authoring this book, there were times where I somewhat felt discouraged—the devil of darkness working overtime to fire shots of discouragement. God told me, "My son, be strong and courageous." I had to meditate more on God's Word and pray in tongues more to get things going. God's Spirit has been teaching, guiding, and encouraging me all along the way.

THE GIFT OF THE HOLY SPIRIT

Remember, I told you before that human beings are spirit beings swathed in a body. Your real self is not your biological body. Your real self is your human spirit. But it surprises me that a lot of people pay so much attention to their bodies and leave their spirits to suffer.

God and His Son, Jesus, are in Heaven. On Earth, we have God's Spirit. But, who is the Holy Spirit? He is the One Who proceeds from God. He has come to live inside your spirit. He mingles with your spirit in such a way that you become one spirit. When you are in Christ, you receive God's Spirit. The Spirit is the Carrier of God's presence. The Spirit is the Doer of God's Word. He is the Power of God. **"Now the Lord is that Spirit . . . "** (2 Cor. 3:17).

The Holy Spirit is the most precious Gift that you could ever receive from God. When all hell breaks loose, He's the One I turn to. He's my best Friend. He helps you with your weaknesses, making intercessions for you according to God's will (Rom. 8:26-27).

He is the Glory of God. He is also the Voice of God—that still, small Voice in your spirit. Some people may say, "It's my conscience." That is the Spirit at work in you. Each time I want to make a wrong decision, He counsels me to say no, even when it is something tremendously appealing.

There was a time when I received a job offer. It was a better job with a bigger salary and better benefits. But the Spirit told me not to accept it. I declined the job offer.

FAITH TO TAKE DOWN STRONGHOLDS

The fight of faith—light against darkness—is not a physical battle but a spiritual one. Darkness creates worldly pressure. If you cannot overcome this pressure, your faith is limited (Prov. 24:10). My friend, we are engaged in spiritual warfare. Faith involves battles that are meant to obliterate demonic strongholds. Any area of your life in which you are held bondage is a stronghold: idolizing money, bitterness, paranoia, laziness, distraction, pride, gossip, sorrow, fornication, adultery, pornography, alcoholism, anger, hatred, shame, lying, poverty, insanity, flirtation, depression, suicidal thoughts, demonic movies, self-pity. The list is almost endless. Please don't allow these things to imprison you. All these things are grossly inconsistent with God's Word.

How do we stop strongholds (darkness)? Strongholds are built when you accept and receive falsehoods and begin to meditate on them or grow up with them. They begin to form a false truth in your psyche, which often becomes a way of life.

I would like to briefly discuss sexual harassment. A lady once told me her story. She got a new job, and her new boss kept on making unwanted advances—touching her inappropriately. The situation got so horrible that she had to quit the job. The problem usually starts from the initiator having sexual thoughts, which later becomes an avalanche of repeated sexual cogitations. There is this urge to fulfill the lust of the flesh.

The stronghold of lust will cause a man or woman to start having sexual thoughts about someone. You begin to nurture wild imaginations. Your mind tells you, "Maybe I'm in love." Really? Can you ask yourself, "What am I really doing?" Yes, she's beautiful. Oh, he's so cute. "I can't really help myself! I just want to be with that person, but just for a moment." What happens after that? Euphoria? Pleasure? Shame? Remorse? Or who's next? There is nothing wrong with seeing a beautiful person, but do not engage in fantasies about him or her. Stop! Just consider that person as brother or sister.

Whether you are a Christian or not, you may face sexual temptation. In Second Samuel 11-12, the legendary King David of Israel—a man after God's heart—lusted after Bathsheba, the wife of Uriah, the Hittite, who was a soldier. When David saw her bathing in her courtyard from the roof of his palace, he just couldn't help himself. David slept with her in Uriah's absence, and she became pregnant. David ordered Uriah to the frontlines of battle, and enemy combatants killed him. The first child born because of David and Bathsheba's infidelity died after seven days.

Despite the sin of murder and adultery, David had the guts to go into repentance mode. He received forgiveness from God. If you are faced with such a situation and want to get out of it, you'll need to incessantly replace those sexual thoughts with God's Word. The times when the thoughts come, resist them, then meditate on and speak God's Word. The origin of the problem is your thought life. Deal with it from the root. If the pressure or urge is colossal, sit down, relax, and pray like this: "Father, in the name of Jesus, my thoughts are pure, noble, right, and excellent. Amen!" Pray like this each time the thoughts come to you.

The apostle Paul noted that the Christians in Galatia were entrapped with fleshly ways. Therefore, he had to admonish the Galatian church:

Now the practices of the sinful nature are *clearly* evident: they are sexual immorality, impurity, sensuality (total

irresponsibility, lack of self-control), idolatry, sorcery, hostility, strife, jealousy, fits of anger, disputes, dissensions, factions [that promote heresies], envy, drunkenness, riotous behavior, and *other* things like these. I warn you beforehand, just as I did previously, that those who practice such things will not inherit the kingdom of God (Gal. 5:19-21 AMP).

Paul knew that Galatian Christians could continue walking in darkness if they did not change their comportment. When you walk in the Spirit, you are less likely to walk in the lusts of your flesh.

FIERY DARTS FROM THE EVIL ONE

The devil is on a mission to massacre, filch, and obliterate you. He is a liar—the liar-in-chief. Don't fall for his satanic deceptions and evil machinations. A lot of people don't know that God's Word is the best weapon to destroy the lies of the enemy. I love how the Master, Jesus, used the Word of God to destroy the devil's lies when He was tempted.

For example, the enemy may plant a thought in your mind that it's better to kill yourself than to continue living in this world. What would be your response? Each time he tries to deceive you, use God's Word as your weapon—your shield of faith.

Sometimes, he brings thoughts to my mind such as, "Are you not tired of attending church services? Just stay home today and relax." I say to him in my spirit that the Bible admonishes, **"Not forsaking the assembling of ourselves together . . . "** (Heb. 10:25). It makes no sense for me to stay at home flipping TV channels. I'd rather choose to exercise godliness, glorify God in church, and fellowship with other Christians. The corporate anointing is greater than individual anointing. Therefore, Jesus said in Matthew 18:20, **"For where two or three are gathered together in my name, there am I in the midst of them."** That usually happens in the church.

CONFESSING GOD'S WORD

Speaking God's Word (confessing, professing, or declaring) is a spiritual principle in the Kingdom of God. It helps to activate your faith.

Your mouth does not only serve the purpose of eating good food or communicating with other people. With your mouth, you make declarations that catapults you unto righteousness. You must speak God's Word more than you eat or talk with other people. Speak it in the morning, in the afternoon, and in the evening. The things of God may appear foolish, but they are wise. Only fools despise wisdom. They do this by rejecting God's Word, thereby perishing.

Are you trying to change a hopeless situation? Can you overcome that situation? Yes, you can. You will have to begin to develop your faith. How do you build your faith? You do it by acting on the Word of God. God's Word is Light. God is in a realm of light that you can only see when you are born into the light. You can see God in His Word.

Are you in the wrong place? God has given you a measure of faith. God is pleased with acts of faith, and faith always works. God is waiting for you to change the situation. Use God's Word to change your situation. God's Word is the testimony. God's Word is your life. Death and life are in your mouth (Prov. 18:21). You will not see a sustained change until you testify of His Word.

DOING THE WORD

It is good to listen to God's Word. But life does not end there. You also must *do* the Word, as we see in James 1:22. How do you do the Word? You simply do what God tells you to do.

For example, the Bible says, **"Rejoice in the Lord always . . . "**(Phil. 4:4), so you must rejoice even when you feel sad.

The Bible says, **"Pray without ceasing"** (1 Thess. 5:17). This means that you must pray regularly, irrespective of how things are going in your life.

The Bible says that you should not forsake the assembly of the brethren (Heb. 10:25). This means you must fellowship with other Christians. Where do Christians meet? They mostly meet in church.

In Genesis twenty-six, we see how God told Isaac to stay in Gerar. There was a dreadful famine in the land, and everybody was fleeing to Egypt to live the Egyptian dream. God told Isaac to stay in the land, and He would bless him and give all the lands to him and his descendants. Isaac sowed in that land; and in the same year, God blessed him with a hundredfold increase. He had flocks and herds and a great household, and he became very wealthy. God's Word was his wisdom. The Bible describes a fool as a person who ignores wisdom (Prov. 12:1). The Bible is replete with God's wisdom. If you choose to turn away from it, you are inviting insanity into your life.

SCRIPTURE REFLECTIONS (NKJV) WITH BRIEF COMMENTARIES

John 1:1: "In the beginning was the Word, and the Word was with God, and the Word was God."

When you read the Bible, consider it as God talking to you. Receive the Word with gladness and meekness.

Psalm 119:114: "You *are* my hiding place and my shield; I hope in Your word."

God's Word is reliable and trustworthy. When there's no light at the end of the tunnel, encourage yourself in the Word.

Psalm 119:133: "Direct my steps by Your word, And let no iniquity have dominion over me."

God's Word is a sure Guide. It gives you instructions on how to live a glorious life.

Psalm 119:147: "I rise before the dawning of the morning, And cry for help; I hope in Your word."

There is nothing that can bless us more than God's engrafted Word. His Word keeps our hopes alive.

John 8:51: "Most assuredly, I say to you, if anyone keeps My word he shall never see death."

God's Word is life. If you trust in the efficacy of God's Word, it would produce life in any situation.

1 John 2:5: "But whoever keeps His word, truly the love of God is perfected in him. By this we know that we are in Him."

God's Word must abide in your spirit. Doing God's Word makes you perfect in God's love.

Ephesians 6:17: "And take the helmet of salvation, and the sword of the Spirit, which is the word of God."

In spiritual warfare, God's Word is a powerful weapon, which is used to destroy the machinations of the evil one.

PRAYER

Father, in the name of Jesus, I thank You, Lord, for the blessing of Your Word. I commit to meditating on Your Word every day so that I will live a prosperous life. I pray that through Your Word, my faith will be activated and my mind renewed. My way of thinking is being transformed from glory to glory, for I have received the Spirit of Truth in God. In the name of Jesus, I pray. Amen.

CONCLUSION

MY EXPECTATION IS THAT THROUGH *The Glory of God's Light,* people will find God, especially at their point of need. Maybe you are upset that you are not making progress in your career, in your business, in your family, in your health, in your relationships, or in your financial goals. Don't be melancholy because I bring glad tidings to encourage you.

Every second, every minute, every hour, there is someone out there experiencing a terrible situation. Is it you? Who can you genuinely trust to deal with your situation? Will you glory in humans? Or will you glory in God? I encourage you to cheer up because God will always care for you.

Our society is so fast-paced that we want everything at the snap of the fingers. Imagine you are way past twenty-five years of age and don't have a college degree; or you are approaching forty years of age and are not married; or you don't own a house or even a nice car. Western society has put tremendous pressure on people, and many are beginning to lose hope. God is your Hope.

There is so much darkness in the world. The forces of darkness are in full operation to ensure that you perish. I felt compelled to start a conversation about God's Light. God does not have any iota of darkness. The light of God's Word is the solution to the problems we face in the world today. I am very passionate about the subject of God's Light. God has given me His Light, and it is my responsibility to share it with the world.

The most important thing in your life is your relationship with God. To build a relationship with God, you must know and trust Him completely with your heart, soul, and mind. Not knowing or trusting God is tantamount to spiritual darkness. I am sure your spiritual eyes have beheld God's glory as a powerful and life-changing reality.

God does not expect you to be perfect in every way before you connect with Him. He loved you first, and your relationship with Him is based on His grace and love for you. You may be in terrible distress and danger, but God is lifting you out of the rubble. His amazing grace is enough to take care of your troubles.

A life fraught with ups and downs is not what God wants for you. The vanities of life are nothing compared to fellowship with God. If you walk in God's Light, Love, and Word, you will always be on top. Through the Spirit, I can see your soul stirred, your spirit refreshed, and your dreams and visions materializing.

I hope this book has blessed you. I want you to enjoy life abundantly. You can start enjoying eternal life here on Earth once you are in Christ. I want you to go to Heaven. I think about Heaven every day. My beloved friend, I want the very best for you.

I hope you have learned something about how you can connect with God. I would encourage you to continue studying God's Word in the Bible because it would light up your life. You must do this regularly so that you mind is renewed and cleansed with the anointing of His Truth.

I wonder what my life would have been without God's Word. I do not know if I would be alive today. I don't know what could have happened in my life. I could be living in darkness. I am sure, if someone tried to tell me about God, I would be indifferent.

I have brought you a message of encouragement today. As a follower of Christ, my standard is not to judge you. If there are areas in the book where you felt that way, it was meant for instruction in righteousness. The ministry of the Word is meant to guide you in the affairs of life.

God is Light. God is Love. God's Light is reflected in His Word. God is inviting you to connect with Him in His Light because He is the Father of

Lights. He wants you to be His very own child of Light. When you receive God's Light, you will be able to transform your life. You will be able to bless others. God's purpose for you is to be the light of the world. God has blessed you and wants you to be an inspiration to the world around you. Arise! Shine! Let your light be manifest.

Darkness depicts anything that is related to the works of the devil—sin, death, negativity, and all forms of evil. The enemy operates in the realm of darkness. God operates in the realm of light. When you truly follow the Lord, it is guaranteed that you will have the light of life and not walk in darkness. You will be catapulted out of the realm of darkness into the realm of His marvelous light (1 Pet. 2:9).

One of the things that can prevent you from walking in the light is unbelief. Jesus went to His hometown and could not do any miracles there, except lay his hands on a few people and heal them (Mk. 6:5). He was stunned at their unbelief. Unbelief is a sin that happens when you refuse to trust and obey God. It is a flawed attitude that blocks people from connecting with God. The panacea for unbelief is God's Word. The more of God's Word you receive in your spirit, the stronger your faith becomes to connect with God.

It is not surprising to find people asking questions such as: "Who is God?" "Is there a God?" "What is He like?" Come to think of it, that is a very important question. You might even be thinking, "Why does God not appear to me?" "Why does He not solve the problems that are going on in the world today?" "Why does He not manifest Himself so that people could know that He exists?"

Do you want to see the glory of God? Moses, a prophet in the Bible, asked God to show him His glory (Exod. 33:18-20). Literally, he meant to say, "Who are you, God?" God, Who is so magnificent in His glory, revealed a part of Himself to Moses, while His glory passed by Moses in a cleft of a rock and covered by God's hand. Another prophet in the Bible, Ezekiel, fell flat on his face when he beheld God's glory (Ezek. 44:4). These prophets of old had unique experiences with God.

It's 2,020 years after the resurrection of Jesus Christ. How do we see God's glory in our time? To see God's glory, you must, first, understand that He is a Spirit. You connect with God through your spirit and not your physical senses—sight, hearing, smell, taste, and touch.

It may appear difficult to relate to an intangible Spirit in the physical realm. But there is a spirit in every human that can connect with God. God has revealed Himself today through the Holy Spirit. The Holy Spirit is the One Who makes God's presence real to you.

The Holy Spirit helps you to know the things that God has freely blessed you with. God has already blessed you. The Holy Spirit also helps to open the eyes of your understanding. He enlightens you in the things of God and reveals to you the realities of the Kingdom of God.

It would be impossible to see God's glory without believing in Jesus Christ, Who is the glory of God's light. The glory of the Lord can be found in His mirror, which is His Word. Through His Word, you will discover the glory of His light and His love.

As you meditate on God's Word, you are transformed. In this process, God's Spirit changes you into the express image of God from glory to glory. You will begin to see the true image of who you really are—a righteous, wise, justified, redeemed, blessed, victorious, and prosperous person.

What you are today reflects what you have been saying over the years past. Negative thoughts and words beget negative results. Good thoughts and words beget good results. I would like to encourage you to talk rightly about your life.

God is telling me to tell you to spend time in prayer every day with Him. He is also saying that you should give thanks to Him every day irrespective of whether times are good or bad. No matter what is going on, give thanks. Don't complain. Even when the evil one throws his best shot at you, just give God thanks.

Do your very best to love God every day just as children cherish every moment spent with their parents. Kindly cherish your Heavenly Father, Who has invoked supernatural blessings upon you and given you His very own Divine life through His Son Jesus Christ.

What is preventing you from connecting with God? Is it unawareness, distress, tragedy, destitution, gloominess, endangerment, or demise? The Lord is moved with compassion for you.

Do you want to know God today? Do you want to see God today? Do you want to connect with God today? Zero in on Jesus. Your life will never be the same again. Even if you don't desire to have a relationship with God, God still wants a relationship with you. What are you going to do when the government, family, or friends can't help your soul? How will you believe in hope against hope? God, on His part, will always love you. Walking with God brings great satisfaction and fulfilment. No matter your problem, no matter the situation, God is here to help. It's time to push that reset button.

For the challenges that you face, you must overcome. For the darkness that you go through, you must activate God's Light. In the glory of God's Light, you shall experience love, bliss, rest, endurance, compassion, virtuousness, truth, calmness, and self-discipline.

You can change any hopeless situation if you have faith in God. Faith simply means believing before seeing through your spiritual eyes. God has given you a measure of faith. However, this is not the end of the story. You are expected to build up your faith. It is like building an edifice. You have a foundation, but you must complete the building right to the top. How does this happen? You must meditate on God's Word as often as possible because you acquire faith by receiving God's Word in your spirit. You must never stop meditating on God's Word, no matter your situation. Faith always works. It never fails. Why then should you worry about your situation? Some people declare their victory in a situation, and after some time, they change their confession if things start taking a negative turn. Be very careful with your tongue because death and life come from what you say.

I would like to pray for you.

> Dear God, in the name Jesus Christ, I release God's supernatural blessings in this person's home, family, finances, job, business, and health. May God's grace be increased in his or her life. Let the spirit of love work in them now and all the rest of their days. Let Your light reign in them. Allow Your Word to abide with them. May the glory of God be with them always. Amen!

LIGHT IS BEAUTIFUL

Light is beautiful.
Light is fabulous.
Light is wonderful.
Light is marvelous.

Light is powerful.
Light is gracious.
Light is merciful.
Light is glorious.

Light is direction.
Light is healing.
Light is correction.
Light is pleasing.

Light is good.
Light is truth.
Light is salvation.
Light is Christ.

Light is sharp.
Light is free.
Light is epiphany.
Light is glee.

THE GIFT OF SALVATION

THE BIBLE TELLS US OF a certain Ethiopian eunuch. The man was a court official of Candace, queen of the Ethiopians. He oversaw all her treasure (like the Treasury Secretary). He came to Jerusalem to worship God. God directed the apostle Philip to join this man in his chariot in the desert. Philip preached Jesus to him. The man received salvation and was baptized by Philip (see Acts 8).

Jesus said, **"Go ye therefore, and teach all nations . . . "** (Matt. 28:19). People will not receive salvation unless someone brings the message of the Gospel to them. The Gospel is God's power that brings complete salvation to you. In Luke 19:10, Jesus said, **"For the Son of man is come to seek and to save that which was lost."** Jesus came to the earth to save the world from sin. He is in Heaven now, and His followers continue to do His work all around the world.

I received salvation when I was about ten years old. I made a declaration to God. To receive Jesus Christ as your Savior, please say this prayer:

Father in the name of Jesus, I turn away from my past. I believe that Your Son, Jesus Christ, died for my sins, was resurrected from the dead, and is alive in Heaven. I accept Jesus Christ as the Lord of my life. He rules and reigns in my heart from this day forward. I receive the Holy Spirit to help me obey You and to do Your will for the rest of my life. In Jesus' name, I pray. Amen.

If you prayed this prayer from your heart and you meant it, you are now born again. Congratulations! You are a follower of Jesus Christ. Even if you don't feel different, you can trust that your eternal salvation is guaranteed as promised in Romans 10:9-10 (AMP):

> **Because if you acknowledge *and* confess with your mouth that Jesus is Lord [recognizing His power, authority, and majesty as God], and believe in your heart that God raised Him from the dead, you will be saved. For with the heart a person believes [in Christ as Savior] resulting in his justification [that is, being made righteous—being freed of the guilt of sin and made acceptable to God]; and with the mouth he acknowledges *and* confesses [his faith openly], resulting in *and* confirming [his] salvation.**

Once you accept with your mouth that Jesus Christ was raised from the dead and proclaim that He is now your Lord and Savior you are automatically free from all sin and made righteous in God through Jesus Christ.

The next step is for you to look for a local Bible-believing church and fellowship there regularly. In church, you will learn more about God, get to love Him, and fellowship with other Christians as well.

LETTER TO THE READER

DEAR READER,

I believe this book has been a heartsome one for you. I believe your spirit has been lifted. I would like to encourage you to read the Bible daily. Study it. Meditate on it every day. You will see the difference it makes in your life.

From my childhood days, God had called me to serve Him. Over the years, I have served Him in different capacities. He had a great plan for my life from the day I accepted Him. I have since walked in my Divine destiny.

One of the things that thrills my soul is writing. My heart is always stirred, and I am ready to write at any time. My penmanship in the Lord continues. I look forward to writing more Christian books in the future.

If God has touched you and you would like to support my work in any way, please send me an email to bro.ray@aol.com.

The grace of our Lord Jesus Christ, the love of God, and the fellowship of the Holy Spirit be with you. Amen!

Yours in Christ,

Brother Raymond

BIBLIOGRAPHY

Bible Hub, s.v. "Christos," Accessed July 5, 2018, http://biblehub.com/greek/5547.htm.

Bible Hub, s.v. "Epignósis," Accessed July 5, 2018, http://biblehub.com/greek/1922.htm.

Bible Hub, s.v. "Gadowl Ma'owr," Accessed January 3, 2018, http://biblehub.com/lexicon/genesis/1-16.htm.

Bible Hub, s.v. "Glōssais Lalein," Accessed January 3, 2018, http://biblehub.com/greek/1100.htm.

Bible Hub, s.v., "Qaton Ma'owr," Accessed January 3, 2018, http://biblehub.com/lexicon/genesis/1-16.htm.

Bible Hub, s.v. "Rhema," Accessed January 3, 2018, http://biblehub.com/greek/4487.htm.

Bible Hub, s.v. "Yehi Or," Accessed January 3, 2018, http://biblehub.com/text/genesis/1-3.htm.

Colman, Andrew (3rd ed.). *A Dictionary of Psychology* (Oxford: University Press, 2009), Accessed January 3, 2018, https://books.google.ca/books?id=UDnvBQAAQBAJ&printsec=frontcover&dq=Andrew+M.+Colman&hl=en&sa=X&ved=0ahUKEwjh8fv8hfLcAhWOTN8KHeMGBnUQ6AEIKjAA#v=onepage&q=Andrew%20M.%20Colman&f=false.

Harry, Boma. The Parchment. Boma Music. I Am Satisfied (Single). 2017. Accessed January 3, 2018, https://www.youtube.com/watch?v=MnL1gw9ypiQ.

ABOUT THE AUTHOR

Brother Raymond is involved in the work of ministry in several capacities—cell ministry leadership, choir, church administration, outreach, and evangelism. He started his walk with God in Sunday school over two decades ago. He is a father, business professional, and instrumentalist (drums and piano). He loves studying the Bible. He and his family live in Canada.

For more information about
Brother Raymond
and
The Glory of God's Light
please contact:

bro.ray@aol.com

For more information about
AMBASSADOR INTERNATIONAL
please connect at:

www.ambassador-international.com
@AmbassadorIntl
www.facebook.com/AmbassadorIntl

If you enjoyed this book, please consider leaving us a review on
Amazon, Goodreads, or our website.